TOP NOTCH

English for Today's World

FUNDAMENTALS

Joan Saslow ■ Allen Ascher

With *Top Notch Pop Songs and Karaoke*
by Rob Morsberger

PEARSON
Longman

Top Notch: English for Today's World   Fundamentals

Pearson Education, 10 Bank Street, White Plains, NY 10606

Editorial director: Pamela Fishman
Senior development editor: Jessica Miller-Smith
Vice president, director of design and production: Rhea Banker
Director of electronic production: Aliza Greenblatt
Managing editor: Mike Kemper
Senior production editor: Sasha Kintzler
Art director: Ann France
Senior manufacturing buyer: Dave Dickey
Photo research: Aerin Csigay
Digital layout specialist: Warren Fischbach
Text composition: Studio Montage
Text font: Palatino 11/13
Cover Photograph: "From Above," by Rhea Banker. Copyright © 2005 Rhea Banker.

Library of Congress Cataloging-in-Publication Data

Saslow, Joan M.
  Top notch : English for today's world. Fundamentals / Joan Saslow, Allen Ascher.
     p. cm.
  1. English language--Textbooks for foreign speakers.   2. English language--Problems, exercises, etc.
     I. Ascher, Allen. II. Title.
PE1128.S27567 2005
428.2'4--dc22   2004059406

ISBN 0-13-184036-3 (pbk. : alk. paper)

Photo credits: All original photography by David Mager; page 4 (1) Dex Images/Corbis, (2) Jose Luis Pelaez, Inc./Corbis, (3) Jim Arbogast/Getty Images, (4) Kim Steele/Getty Images, (5) Mark Richards/PhotoEdit, (6) Getty Images, (7) Jose Luis Pelaez, Inc./Corbis, (8) Getty Images, (9) Royalty-Free/Corbis, (10) Getty Images, (11) Reuters NewMedia Inc./Corbis, (12) Kevin Winter/Getty Images; p. 5 (left) Robert Mora/Getty Images, (center left) Sonora, Inc., (center right) Reuters NewMedia Inc./Corbis, (right) Piero Pomponi/Liaison/Getty Images; p. 6 (1) Alan Bolesta/Index Stock Imagery, (2) Tom McCarthy/PhotoEdit, (3) Spencer Grant/PhotoEdit, (4) James P. Blair/Corbis, (5) Getty Images, (6) Thinkstock, (7) Royalty-Free/Corbis, (8) Getty Images; p. 10 (top left) Jose Luis Pelaez, Inc./Corbis, (top middle) Jose Luis Pelaez, Inc./Corbis, (top right) Dex Images/Corbis, (bottom left) Dex Images/Corbis, (bottom middle) Royalty-Free/Corbis, (bottom right) Getty Images; p. 18 (map) Hammond World Atlas Corporation, (Travolta) Rob Griffith/AP Wide World, (Ma) Jessica Griffin/AP Wide World, (Pei) Owen Franken/Corbis, (Fernandez) Reuters NewMedia Inc./Corbis, (Allende) Szenes Jason/Corbis Sygma, (Jaffrey) Azzara Steve/Corbis Sygma; p. 20 (1) Bill Aron/PhotoEdit, (2) Getty Images, (3) Tom Carter/PhotoEdit, (4) Bill Bachmann/PhotoEdit, (5) Steven Dunwell/Getty Images, (6) Jeff Greenberg/PhotoEdit, (7) Michael Newman/PhotoEdit, (8) Dave Bartruff/Corbis; p. 22 (left) John Elk III, (middle) Robert Frerck/Odyssey, (right) Jeff Greenberg/PhotoEdit; p. 24 (1) William Taufic/Corbis, (2) Dave G. Houser/Corbis, (3) Robert Frerck/Odyssey, (4) Mimmo Jodice/Corbis, (5) James Leynse/Corbis; p. 26 (left) Bohemian Nomad Picturemakers/Corbis, (middle) Robert Frerck/Woodfin Camp & Associates, (right) Takanori Yamakawa/Pacific Press Service; p. 28 (tree) Rosemary Calvert/ImageState; p. 28 (1 left) Steve Casimiro/Getty Images, (1 right) Myrleen Ferguson Cate/PhotoEdit, (2 left) Mark Richards/PhotoEdit, (2 right) Myrleen Ferguson Cate/PhotoEdit, (3 left) Royalty-Free/Corbis, (3 right) Steve Smith/SuperStock, (4 left) Nathan Michaels/SuperStock, (4 right) Mark Richards/PhotoEdit, (5 left) David Lees/Getty Images, (5 right) Michael Newman/PhotoEdit, (6 left) Getty Images, (6 right) Jim Whitmer Photography; p. 32 (1) Douglas Kirkland/Corbis, (2) Lisa O'Connor/ZUMA/Corbis, (4) Rick Gomez/Masterfile, (5&6) Universal/The Kobal Collection, (7) Alpha Photo Press Agency Ltd./Globe Photos, (8) Corbis Sygma; p. 34 (left) Reuters NewMedia Inc./Corbis, (middle) Elise Amendola/AP Wide World, (right) Kevork Djansezian/AP Wide World; p. 35 (top) David Lok/SuperStock, (bottom) Darama/Corbis; p. 38 (1 inset) Original Films/The Kobal Collection, (1) Graham French/Masterfile, (2) Robbie Jack Photography, (3) Stephanie Maze/Corbis, (4) Alamy Images, (5) AFP/Corbis, (6) Getty Images; p. 39 (Jaffrey) Azzara Steve/Corbis Sygma; p. 44 (1) Dorling Kindersley, (2) www.canz.biz, (3) Dorling Kindersley, (4) www.canz.biz, (5) Andersen Ross/Getty Images, (6) FashionSyndicatePress.com, (7) Carin Krasner/Corbis, (8&9) Getty Images, (10) FashionSyndicatePress.com; p. 47 (sweater) Michael Newman/PhotoEdit, (woman's suit) Dorling Kindersley, (man's suit) Dorling Kindersley, (man's shoes) Michael Newman/PhotoEdit, (pants) David Young-Wolff/PhotoEdit, (tie) Richard Hutchings/PhotoEdit, (man's shoes) David Young-Wolff/PhotoEdit; p. 49 (shoes) Michael Newman/PhotoEdit, (tie) www.canz.biz, (shirt) www.canz.biz, (man) FashionSyndicatePress.com, (woman) FashionSyndicatePress.com; p. 50 (sweaters) Ted Morrison/SuperStock, (man's shoe) Dorling Kindersley, (woman's shoes) Dorling Kindersley; p. 55 (top) Getty Images; p. 57 (leather chair) LonHarding.com, (chair) Museum of Fine Arts, Houston, Texas, USA./Bridgeman Art Library, Gift of Dr. and Mrs. Peter Marzio, (lamp) Peter Harholdt/Corbis, (rug) Jacqui Hurst/Corbis, (red couch) Christie's Images Inc., (couch) Christie's Images Inc.; p. 74 (top) iRobot Corporation, (right) Husqvarna (U.S. Corporate Offices), (bottom) AFP/Corbis; p. 76 Gala/SuperStock; p. 85 (soup) Getty Images, (bean salad) Lisa Koenig/Stockfood America, (pancakes) Getty Images, (peppers) Solzberg Studio/Stockfood America; p. 94 (top) Photolibrary.com, (middle) Dave G. Houser/Corbis, (bottom) Fraser Hall/Robert Harding World Imagery; p. 95 (1) Bill Bachmann/Mira.com, (2) Michael Keller/Corbis, (3) Getty Images, (4) Norbert Schaefer/Corbis, (5) Tim Kiusalaas/Corbis, (6) Alamy Images; p. 96 Dennis MacDonald/PhotoEdit; p. 97 (Rome) Dallas and John Heaton/Corbis, (London) Ric Ergenbright/Corbis, (Rio) Pat Canova/Index Stock Imagery, (Moscow) H. Spichtinger/Masterfile, (Kong) Reed Kaestner/Corbis, (Hawaii) Randy Faris/Corbis, (Istanbul) Brian Lawrence/SuperStock; p. 98 (café) Catherine Karnow/Corbis, (Louvre) Walter Bibikow/Index Stock Imagery, (Tower) Royalty-Free/Corbis, (Cancun) Michele Westmorland/Corbis, (snorkeling) Mike Severns/Getty Images, (Tulum) Steve Vidler/eStock Photo, (ferry) Getty Images, (sum) Nik Wheeler/Corbis; p. 100 (3) Getty Images, (5) Getty Images, (6) Getty Images; p. 101 (Mercury) Manny Hernandez/Liaison/Getty Images, (Fat) Corbis Sygma, (Boccelli) Mencarini/Grazia Neri/Corbis Sygma, (Miguel) David Sprague/LADN/WireImage.com, (Ming) AFP/Corbis, (Binoche) Reuters NewMedia Inc./Corbis; p. 106 (Depardieu) Eric Fougere/VIP Images/Corbis, (Yi) Reuters NewMedia Inc./Corbis, (Veloso) Wrasse Records, (Reiner) Frederick M. Brown/Getty Images, (Roberts) Andrea Renault/Globe Photos; p. 111 (top left) Robert Frerck and Odyssey Productions, Inc., (middle) Bill Aron/PhotoEdit, (top right) Dave G. Houser/Corbis, (bottom left) Dennis Degnan/Corbis, (bottom right) Mimmo Jodice/Corbis; p.117 (1) Peter Beck/Corbis, (2) ATC Productions/Corbis, (3) Jose Luis Pelaez, Inc./Corbis, (4) Jose Luis Pelaez, Inc./Corbis, (5) Tom & Dee Ann McCarthy/Corbis, (6) Jose Luis Pelaez, Inc./Corbis, (7) Andrew Douglas/Masterfile, (8) Getty Images, (9) Michael Keller/Corbis, (10) Billy E. Barnes/PhotoEdit; p. 122 (Thor) Walter Leonardi, (Kon-Tiki) Getty Images; p. V1 (Unit 1) (2) Picture Quest/Jim Pickerell/Stock Connection, (3) Keith Brofsky/Getty Images, (4) Arthur S. Aubry/Getty Images, (5) Royalty-Free/Corbis, (9) Kwame Zikomo/SuperStock, (10) Royalty-Free/Corbis, (12) Jonathan Nouvok/Image Works, (16) Comstock Images, (Unit 2) (1&2) Corbis, (3) Doug Pensinger/Getty Images, (4) Royalty-Free/Corbis, (5) John Henley/Corbis, (6) Roger Ressmeyer/Corbis; p. V2 (Unit 3) (4) Vittoriano Rastelli/Corbis, (5) Corbis, (6) Corbis, (7) Corbis, (8) Tom & Dee Ann McCarthy/Corbis, (9) Tom Wagner/Corbis Saba, (10) Jeff Greenberg/PhotoEdit, (11) Getty Images, (Unit 4) (1) Dorling Kindersley, (2) Duane Rieder, (3) Dorling Kindersley, (Unit 5) (1) Dorling Kindersley, (2) Corbis, (3) Dorling Kindersley, (5) Kazuhiro Nogi/AFP/Getty Images, (p. V3 (3) Dorling Kindersley, (4) Comstock Images; p. V4 (19) Dorling Kindersley; p. V5 (Unit 8) (1) PhotoEdit/Robert Brenner; p. V6 (1) A&J Verkaik/Corbis, (2) Michael S. Yamashita/Corbis, (3) Annie Griffiths Belt/National Geographic Image Collection, (4) Frozen Images/The Image Works; p. V7 (Unit 11) (2) Royalty-Free/Corbis, (3) Comstock Images, (4) Jim Cummins/Getty Images, (5) Royalty-Free/Corbis, (6) Royalty-Free/Corbis, (8) Royalty-Free/Corbis; p. V8 (Unit 12) (top left) Michael Keller/Corbis, (top right) Dorling Kindersley, (Unit 13) (1-11, 13) Dorling Kindersley, (12) Getty Images; p. V9 (Unit 14) (1) Douglas Faulkner/Corbis, (2) Rich Iwasaki/AGE Fotostock America, Inc., (3) Phil Schermeister/Corbis, (4) Francoise DeMulder/Corbis, (5) Jennifer W. Lester, (More) (1) Royalty-Free/Corbis, (2) Pixtal/SuperStock, (3) Royalty-Free/Corbis, (4) Tony Anderson/Getty Images, (5) Gisela Damm/eStock Photo, (6) ThinkStock/SuperStock.

Illustration credits: Kenneth Bateman: pp. 21 (bottom), 23, 24, 25, 48 (bottom), 52, 54, 61, 64; Sue Carlson: p. 53; John Ceballos: pp. 11, 19, 27, 43, 51, 59, 67, 75, 83, 91, 99, 107, 115, 123; Jim Delapine: p. 36; Scott Fray: pp. 56, 84, 87; Mona Mark: p. 90; Andy Myer: pp. 7, 17, 45 (bottom); Sandy Nichols: pp. 6, 37, 79; Dusan Petricic: pp. 8, 44, 45 (top), 62, 76, 78, 102 (middle), 104 (top), 105, 116, 126, 130; Mike Reagan: p.122; Phil Scheuer: pp. 2, 70, 95 (top), 102 (bottom), 103, 104 (bottom), 108 (top), 109, 110 (bottom), 111, 118, 120, 121 (right); Don Stewart: pp. 48 (top), 102 (top); Neil Stewart: pp. 20, 21 (top), 22, 23 (top), 36, 40, 52 (bottom), 60, 69; Meryl Treatner: p. 114; Chris Vallo: p. 10; Anna Veltfort: pp. 12, 30, 60, 68, 78 (top), 88, 93, 95 (bottom), 108 (bottom), 110 (top), 112, 121 (left), 124, 129.

Text credit: Recipes on page 90: Copyright © 1997 by Rozanne Gold. Reprinted by permission of William Morris Agency, Inc., on behalf of the Author.

Printed in the United States of America
2 3 4 5 6 7 8 9 10–CRK–10 09 08 07 06 05

Contents

Scope and Sequence OF CONTENT AND SKILLS

UNIT	Vocabulary	Vocabulary Booster	Social Language	Grammar
1 **Names and Occupations** *Page 4*	• Occupations • The alphabet	• More occupations	• Talk about what you do • Identify people • Politely begin a conversation • Spell names	• <u>Be</u>: singular statements • Singular and plural nouns • <u>Be</u>: plural statements • <u>Be</u>: <u>yes</u> / <u>no</u> questions and short answers • Proper nouns and common nouns
2 **Relationships** *Page 12* *Top Notch* Song: "Excuse Me, Please"	• Relationships • Titles and names • Numbers 0–20	• More relationships • More titles	• Introduce people • Tell someone your first and last name • Get someone's address and phone number • Confirm information	• Possessive adjectives and nouns • <u>Be</u>: information questions with <u>What</u>
3 **Directions and Transportation** *Page 20*	• Places in the community • Locations and directions • Means of transportation	• More places in the community	• Ask about the location of places • Give and get directions • Suggest a means of transportation	• <u>Be</u>: questions with <u>Where</u> • Subject pronoun <u>it</u> • <u>There is</u> • The imperative
4 **People** *Page 28* *Top Notch* Song: "Tell Me All about It"	• Family members • Numbers 20–100 • Adjectives to describe people	• More adjectives to describe people	• Ask who someone is • Identify family members • Talk about your family • Ask about someone's age • Describe people	• <u>Be</u>: questions with <u>Who</u> • <u>Have</u> / <u>has</u>: affirmative statements • <u>Be</u>: questions with <u>How old</u> • Adjectives • <u>Very</u> and <u>so</u>
5 **Events and Times** *Page 36*	• Time • Early, <u>on time</u>, <u>late</u> • Events • Days of the week • Months of the year • Ordinal numbers	• More events	• Talk about time • Ask if you are late • Reassure someone • Invite someone to an event • Suggest a time to meet • Talk about dates • Ask about birthdays	• <u>Be</u>: questions about time • Prepositions of time and place
6 **Clothes** *Page 44*	• Clothes • Verbs <u>want</u>, <u>have</u>, <u>need</u> • Colors and other descriptive adjectives	• More clothes	• Give and accept compliments about clothes • Compare opinions about clothes • Talk about shopping for clothes • Describe clothes • Talk about wants and needs	• <u>This</u>, <u>that</u>, <u>these</u>, <u>those</u> • The simple present tense: affirmative statements • The simple present tense: statements and <u>yes</u> / <u>no</u> questions • Adjectives • The simple present tense: information questions
7 **Home and Work** *Page 52*	• Workplaces and homes • Rooms in the home • Furniture and appliances in the home and office	• More home and office vocabulary	• Talk about where you live, work, or study • Describe your home • Compare opinions	• Prepositions of place • <u>There is</u> and <u>There are</u> • <u>A lot of</u>

Speaking Activities	Pronunciation	Listening	Reading and Writing
• Read letters of the alphabet aloud • Spelling bee: Say and spell occupations	• Syllables	• List of letters Task: Circle the letter you hear • Conversations about names Task: Identify correct spelling and write each name • Lists of and conversations about occupations Task: Identify the correct occupation • Conversations about names and occupations Task: Listen for and write missing information	Reading • Names and occupations • Simple forms and business cards Writing • Write proper and common nouns • Complete a form with name and occupation • Write responses to statements and questions
• Ask for someone's first and last name in order to fill out a form • Read aloud a series of numbers for a partner to write • Ask and answer questions about occupations, phone numbers, addresses, and country of origin	• Stress in two-word pairs	• Introductions Task: Listen for and write relationships • Questions about first and last names Task: Circle the first or last name • Conversations about names and phone numbers Task: Write the phone number	Reading • Article about famous people, their occupations, and country of origin Writing • Fill in a form with your first name, last name, title • Fill in a form with a partner's first name and last name • Write telephone numbers from a listening
• Use a map to give location or directions • Give directions to places in your city or town	• Rising intonation to confirm	• List of places in the community Task: Number the places • Conversations about directions Task: Write the name of the place	Reading • Guide to museums around the world Writing • Write questions and answers about location • Write names of places from a listening • Write directions • List places in your city or town • Answer questions about a reading
• Read aloud numbers for a partner to circle • Interview a partner about his or her family	• Numbers	• Identifications of family members Task: Identify the correct person • Conversations describing family members Task: Identify the adjectives used for each	Reading • Article about famous people and their families Writing • Write questions with Who • Interview a partner and write about his or her family
• Discuss times, using a time-zone map • Say and write dates with a partner • Ask about classmates' birthdays	• Sentence stress	• Conversations about events Task: Identify the time of each event • A radio broadcast of upcoming events Task: Write events on a calendar, under correct day and time • List of dates Task: Circle the dates on a calendar	Reading • Newspaper entertainment section Writing • Write events on a calendar • Write dates as a partner says them • Answer questions, using prepositions of time and place • Write classmates' names
• Describe a partner's likes and dislikes • Discuss clothing you need, like, want, or have	• Plural nouns	• Conversations about clothing: likes, wants, needs Task: Identify statements as true or false	Reading • Newspaper ad for a sale at a clothing store Writing • Write names of clothes with this, that, these, or those • Write descriptions of clothes
• Talk about homes that you like and why	• Th	• Phone conversations about houses and apartments Task: Identify the best home for each person • Questions about furniture and appliances Task: Write the correct room for each item	Reading • Newspaper ads for houses and apartments • Descriptions of people's homes Writing • Write a description of a dream house • Write the furniture and appliances in your home • Write comparisons of your home and homes in a reading

Scope and Sequence OF CONTENT AND SKILLS

UNIT	Vocabulary	Vocabulary Booster	Social Language	Grammar
8 **Activities** *Page 68* *Top Notch* Song: "On the Weekend"	• Daily activities at home • Household chores and leisure activities	• More household chores	• Describe your daily activities • Tell why you are a morning person or an evening person • Describe your schedule • Talk about how often you do things • Greet an acquaintance you haven't seen in a while	• The simple present tense: spelling rules for the third-person singular • The simple present tense: habitual activities • Questions with <u>How often</u> • Frequency adverbs
9 **Weather and Ongoing Activities** *Page 76*	• Weather • Time expressions	• More weather	• Ask about the weather • Describe today's weather • Ask about people's activities • Make a polite phone call • Offer to call back later • Discuss plans • Make plans to get together	• The present continuous: affirmative and negative statements • The present continuous: <u>yes</u> / <u>no</u> questions • The present continuous: information questions • The present participle: spelling rules • The present continuous: continuing activities and future plans
10 **Food** *Page 84*	• Foods: count nouns • Places to keep food in a kitchen • Drinks and foods: non-count nouns • Containers and quantities	• More vegetables • More fruits	• Get ingredients for a recipe • Discuss what to cook • Offer and ask for foods at the table • Talk about present-time activities • Invite someone to join you	• <u>How many</u> and <u>Are there any</u> • Non-count nouns • <u>How much</u> and <u>Is there any</u> • The present continuous and the simple present tense
11 **Past Events** *Page 92* *Top Notch* Song: "My Favorite Day"	• Past-time expressions • Years • Weekend activities • Seasons	• More weekend activities	• Talk about the past • Express regret • Discuss past activities • Ask about and describe a vacation	• The past tense of <u>be</u> • The simple past tense • The simple past tense: questions
12 **Appearance and Health** *Page 100*	• Adjectives to describe hair • The face • Parts of the body • Accidents and injuries • Ailments • Remedies	• More parts of the body	• Describe people • Ask about someone who looks familiar • Show concern about an injury • Talk about an ailment • Suggest a remedy	• Use of adjectives for physical description • <u>Should</u> for advice
13 **Abilities and Requests** *Page 108*	• Abilities and skills • Adverbs to describe ability • Reasons to decline an invitation • Requests	• More musical instruments	• Discuss abilities • Decline an invitation • Request a favor	• <u>Can</u> and <u>can't</u> • <u>Too</u> + adjective • Requests with <u>Could</u> or <u>Can</u>
14 **Past, Present, and Future Plans** *Page 116* *Top Notch* Song: "I Wasn't Born Yesterday"	• Academic subjects • Life events • Free-time activities	• More academic subjects • More free-time activities	• Get to know someone's life story • Talk about where you were born • Announce good news and bad news • Congratulate someone • Ask about free-time activities • Ask about future plans	• <u>Would like</u> • <u>Be going to</u> for the future • Conditions and results in the future

Speaking Activities	Pronunciation	Listening	Reading and Writing
• Interview a partner about daily activities • Discuss how often you do things and report to the class • Talk about likes and wants in the context of a reading on robots who do housework	• Third-person singular verbs in the simple present tense	• Conversations about household chores Task: Identify the correct choice to complete sentences • Interviews about transportation Task: Complete a chart, identifying how each person gets to work or school	Reading • Article about robots that perform household chores Writing • Write sentences about daily activities • Write about a partner's daily activities • Fill in a weekly schedule • Write sentences about habitual activities • Write sentences about a reading, using the simple present tense
• Describe the weather • Ask and answer questions about activities in progress now • Charades: ask questions in the present continuous • Make plans to meet	• Rising and falling intonation of questions	• World weather broadcast Task: Write the weather and temperature for each city • Conversations about actions in progress Task: Complete sentences	Reading • A weekly date book • Instant messages Writing • Fill in a weekly date book • Write sentences about your future plans
• Ask and answer questions with How many and Are there any • Create and describe a recipe	• Vowel sounds	• Conversations about food Task: Identify the foods in each	Reading • Recipes • Weekly schedule Writing • Complete a chart with things you eat and drink • Write sentences about activities in progress and habitual activities • Write ingredients for your own recipe
• Tell a partner what you did yesterday • Discuss your favorite season • Ask questions about past activities • Talk about where you want to go on vacation • Describe a vacation you took	• The simple past tense ending	• List of years Task: Identify the correct year • Conversations about events Task: Complete sentences about the day or month of each event	Reading • Descriptions of vacations Writing • Write sentences about past activities • Write sentences to answer questions about a reading • Write a description of a past vacation
• Game: Practice "Parts of the body" vocabulary • Guessing game: describe a classmate	• Back-vowel sounds	• Descriptions of hair Task: Identify the people described • Conversations about injuries Task: Write the injuries • Conversations about ailments Task: Identify the ailments	Reading • Descriptions of people Writing • Write sentences suggesting remedies • Write a description of a classmate
• Describe your abilities • Discuss things children can and can't do at different ages	• Can and can't	• Requests Task: Identify the picture to match each request	Reading • Article about infant and toddler abilities Writing • Write sentences with too and an adjective • Complete sentences about abilities, based on a reading
• Interview a partner about his or her past • Compare plans for the future • Present a short history of your life	• Diphthongs	• An interview about someone's childhood Task: Check the statements that are true • Conversations about future free-time activities Task: Complete sentences with the activities	Reading • Article about Thor Heyerdahl Writing • Write about a partner's life story • Write statements about future plans • Write statements and questions with be going to • Write sentences about a partner's future plans • Write answers to questions, based on a reading • Write a short history of your life

Acknowledgments

Top Notch International Advisory Board

The authors gratefully acknowledge the substantive and formative contributions of the members of the International Advisory Board.

CHERYL BELL, Middlesex County College, Middlesex, New Jersey, USA • **ELMA CABAHUG**, City College of San Francisco, San Francisco, California, USA • **JO CARAGATA**, Mukogawa Women's University, Hyogo, Japan • **ANN CARTIER**, Palo Alto Adult School, Palo Alto, California, USA • **TERRENCE FELLNER**, Himeji Dokkyo University, Hyogo, Japan • **JOHN FUJIMORI**, Meiji Gakuin High School, Tokyo, Japan • **ARETA ULHANA GALAT**, Escola Superior de Estudos Empresariais e Informática, Curitiba, Brazil • **DOREEN M. GAYLORD**, Kanazawa Technical College, Ishikawa, Japan • **EMILY GEHRMAN**, Newton International College, Garden Grove, California, USA • **ANN-MARIE HADZIMA**, National Taiwan University, Taipei, Taiwan • **KAREN KYONG-AI PARK**, Seoul National University, Seoul, Korea • **ANA PATRICIA MARTÍNEZ VITE DIP. R.S.A.**, Universidad del Valle de México, Mexico City, Mexico • **MICHELLE ANN MERRITT**, Proulex/ Universidad de Guadalajara, Guadalajara, Mexico • **ADRIANNE P. OCHOA**, Georgia State University, Atlanta, Georgia, USA • **LOUIS PARDILLO**, Korea Herald English Institute, Seoul, Korea • **THELMA PERES**, Casa Thomas Jefferson, Brasilia, Brazil • **DIANNE RUGGIERO**, Broward Community College, Davie, Florida, USA • **KEN SCHMIDT**, Tohoku Fukushi University, Sendai, Japan • **ALISA A. TAKEUCHI**, Garden Grove Adult Education, Garden Grove, California, USA • **JOSEPHINE TAYLOR**, Centro Colombo Americano, Bogotá, Colombia • **PATRICIA VECIÑO**, Instituto Cultural Argentino Norteamericano, Buenos Aires, Argentina • **FRANCES WESTBROOK**, AUA Language Center, Bangkok, Thailand

Reviewers and Piloters

Many thanks also to the reviewers and piloters all over the world who reviewed *Top Notch* in its final form.

G. Julian Abaqueta, Huachiew Chalermprakiet University, Samutprakarn, Thailand • **David Aline**, Kanagawa University, Kanagawa, Japan • **Marcia Alves**, Centro Cultural Brasil Estados Unidos, Franca, Brazil • **Yousef Al-Yacoub**, Qatar Petroleum, Doha, Qatar • **Maristela Barbosa Silveira e Silva**, Instituto Cultural Brasil-Estados Unidos, Manaus, Brazil • **Beth Bartlett**, Centro Colombo Americano, Cali, Colombia • **Carla Battigelli**, University of Zulia, Maracaibo, Venezuela • **Claudia Bautista**, C.B.C., Caracas, Venezuela • **Rob Bell**, Shumei Yachiyo High School, Chiba, Japan • **Dr. Maher Ben Moussa**, Sharjah University, Sharjah, United Arab Emirates • **Elaine Cantor**, Englewood Senior High School, Jacksonville, Florida, USA • **María Aparecida Capellari**, SENAC, São Paulo, Brazil • **Eunice Carrillo Ramos**, Colegio Durango, Naucalpan, Mexico • **Janette Carvalhinho de Oliveira**, Centro de Linguas (UFES), Vitória, Brazil • **María Amelia Carvalho Fonseca**, Centro Cultural Brasil-Estados Unidos, Belém, Brazil • **Audy Castañeda**, Instituto Pedagógico de Caracas, Caracas, Venezuela • **Ching-Fen Chang**, National Chiao Tung University, Hsinchu, Taiwan • **Ying-Yu Chen**, Chinese Culture University, Taipei, Taiwan • **Joyce Chin**, The Language Training and Testing Center, Taipei, Taiwan • **Eun Cho**, Pagoda Language School, Seoul, Korea • **Hyungzung Cho**, MBC Language Institute, Seoul, Korea • **Dong Sua Choi**, MBC Language Institute, Seoul, Korea • **Jeong Mi Choi**, Freelancer, Seoul, Korea • **Peter Chun**, Pagoda Language School, Seoul, Korea • **Eduardo Corbo**, Legacy ELT, Salto, Uruguay • **Marie Cosgrove**, Surugadai University, Saitama, Japan • **María Antonieta Covarrubias Souza**, Centro Escolar Akela, Mexico City, Mexico • **Katy Cox**, Casa Thomas Jefferson, Brasilia, Brazil • **Michael Donovan**, Gakushuin University, Tokyo, Japan • **Stewart Dorward**, Shumei Eiko High School, Saitama, Japan • **Ney Eric Espina**, Centro Venezolano Americano del Zulia, Maracaibo, Venezuela • **Edith Espino**, Centro Especializado de Lenguas - Universidad Tecnológica de Panamá, El Dorado, Panama • **Allen P. Fermon**, Instituto Brasil-Estados Unidos, Ceará, Brazil • **Simão Ferreira Banha**, Phil Young's English School, Curitiba, Brazil • **María Elena Flores Lara**, Colegio Mercedes, Mexico City, Mexico • **Valesca Fróis Nassif**, Associação Cultural Brasil-Estados Unidos, Salvador, Brazil • **José Fuentes**, Empire Language Consulting, Caracas, Venezuela • **José Luis Guerrero**, Colegio Cristóbal Colón, Mexico City, Mexico • **Claudia Patricia Gutiérrez**, Centro Colombo Americano, Cali, Colombia • **Valerie Hansford**, Asia University, Tokyo, Japan • **Gene Hardstark**, Dotkyo University, Saitama, Japan • **Maiko Hata**, Kansai University, Osaka, Japan • **Susan Elizabeth Haydock Miranda de Araujo**, Centro Cultural Brasil Estados Unidos, Belém, Brazil • **Gabriela Herrera**, Fundametal, Valencia, Venezuela • **Sandy Ho**, GEOS International, New York, New York, USA • **Yuri Hosoda**, Showa Women's University, Tokyo, Japan • **Hsiao-I Hou**, Shu-Te University, Kaohsiung County, Taiwan • **Kuei-ping Hsu**, National Tsing Hua University, Hsinchu, Taiwan • **Chia-yu Huang**, National Tsing Hua University, Hsinchu, Taiwan • **Caroline C. Hwang**, National Taipei University of Science and Technology, Taipei, Taiwan • **Diana Jones**, Angloamericano, Mexico City, Mexico • **Eunjeong Kim**, Freelancer, Seoul, Korea • **Julian Charles King**, Qatar Petroleum, Doha, Qatar • **Bruce Lee**, CIE: Foreign Language Institute, Seoul, Korea • **Myunghee Lee**, MBC Language Institute, Seoul, Korea • **Naidnapa Leoprasertkul**, Language Development Center, Mahasarakham University, Mahasarakham, Thailand • **Eleanor S. Leu**, Souchow University, Taipei, Taiwan • **Eliza Liu**, Chinese Culture University, Taipei, Taiwan • **Carlos Lizárraga**, Angloamericano, Mexico City, Mexico • **Philippe Loussarevian**, Keio University Shonan Fujisawa High School, Kanagawa, Japan • **Jonathan Lynch**, Azabu University, Tokyo, Japan • **Thomas Mach**, Konan University, Hyogo, Japan • **Lilian Mandel Civatti**, Associação Cultural Brasil-Estados Unidos, Salvador, Brazil • **Hakan Mansuroglu**, Zoni Language Center, West New York, New Jersey, USA • **Martha McGaughey**, Language Training Institute, Englewood Cliffs, New Jersey, USA • **David Mendoza Plascencia**, Instituto Internacional de Idiomas, Naucalpan, Mexico • **Theresa Mezo**, Interamerican University, Río Piedras, Puerto Rico • **Luz Adriana Montenegro Silva**, Colegio CAFAM, Bogotá, Colombia • **Magali de Moraes Menti**, Instituto Lingua, Porto Alegre, Brazil • **Massoud Moslehpour**, The Overseas Chinese Institute of Technology, Taichung, Taiwan • **Jennifer Nam**, IKE, Seoul, Korea • **Marcos Norelle F. Victor**, Instituto Brasil-Estados Unidos, Ceará, Brazil • **Luz María Olvera**, Instituto Juventud del Estado de México, Naucalpan, Mexico • **Roxana Orrego Ramírez**, Universidad Diego Portales, Santiago, Chile • **Ming- Jong Pan**, National Central University, Jhongli City, Taiwan • **Sandy Park**, Topia Language School, Seoul, Korea • **Patrícia Elizabeth Peres Martins**, Instituto Brasil-Estados Unidos, Rio de Janeiro, Brazil • **Rodrigo Peza**, Passport Language Centers, Bogotá, Colombia • **William Porter**, Osaka Institute of Technology, Osaka, Japan • **Caleb Prichard**, Kwansei Gakuin University, Hyogo, Japan • **Mirna Quintero**, Instituto Pedagógico de Caracas, Caracas, Venezuela • **Roberto Rabbini**, Seigakuin University, Saitama, Japan • **Terri Rapoport**, Berkeley College, White Plains, New York, USA • **Yvette Rieser**, Centro Electrónico de Idiomas, Maracaibo, Venezuela • **Orlando Rodríguez**, New English Teaching School, Paysandu, Uruguay • **Mayra Rosario**, Pontificia Universidad Católica Madre y Maestra, Santiago, Dominican Republic • **Peter Scout**, Sakura no Seibo Junior College, Fukushima, Japan • **Jungyeon Shim**, EG School, Seoul, Korea • **Keum Ok Song**, MBC Language Institute, Seoul, Korea • **Assistant Professor Dr. Reongrudee Soonthornmanee**, Chulalongkorn University Language Institute, Bangkok, Thailand • **Claudia Stanislause**, The Language College, Maracay, Venezuela • **Tom Suh**, The Princeton Review, Seoul, Korea • **Phiphawin Suphawat**, KhonKaen University, KhonKaen, Thailand • **Craig Sweet**, Poole Gakuin Junior and Senior High Schools, Osaka, Japan • **Yi-nien Josephine Twu**, National Tsing Hua University, Hsinchu, Taiwan • **Maria Christina Uchôa Close**, Instituto Cultural Brasil-Estados Unidos, São José dos Campos, Brazil • **Luz Vanegas Lopera**, Lexicom The Place For Learning English, Medellín, Colombia • **Julieta Vasconcelos García**, Centro Escolar del Lago, A.C., Mexico City, Mexico • **Carol Vaughan**, Kanto Kokusai High School, Tokyo, Japan • **Patricia Celia Veciño**, Instituto Cultural Argentino Norteamericano, Buenos Aires, Argentina • **Isabela Villas Boas**, Casa Thomas Jefferson, Brasilia, Brazil • **Iole Vitti**, Peanuts English School, Poços de Caldas, Brazil • **Gabi Witthaus**, Qatar Petroleum, Doha, Qatar • **Yi-Ling Wu**, Shih Chien University, Taipei, Taiwan • **Chad Wynne**, Osaka Keizai University, Osaka, Japan • **Belkis Yanes**, Freelance Instructor, Caracas, Venezuela • **I-Chieh Yang**, Chung-kuo Institute of Technology, Taipei, Taiwan • **Emil Ysona**, Instituto Cultural Dominico-Americano, Santo Domingo, Dominican Republic • **Chi-fang Yu**, Soo Chow University, Taipei, Taiwan, • **Shigeki Yusa**, Sendai Shirayuri Women's College, Sendai, Japan

To the Teacher

What is *Top Notch*?

- *Top Notch* is a six-level communicative English course for adults and young adults, with two beginning entry levels.
- *Top Notch* prepares students to interact successfully and confidently with both native and non-native speakers of English.
- *Top Notch* demonstrably brings students to a "Top Notch" level of communicative competence.

Key Elements of the *Top Notch* Instructional Design

Concise two-page lessons

Each easy-to-teach two-page lesson is designed for one class session and begins with a clearly stated communication goal and ends with controlled or free communication practice. Each lesson provides vocabulary, grammar, and social language contextualized in all four skills, keeping the pace of a class session lively and varied.

Daily confirmation of progress

Adult and young adult students need to observe and confirm their own progress. In *Top Notch*, students conclude each class session with a controlled or free practice activity that demonstrates their ability to use new vocabulary, grammar, and social language. This motivates and keeps students eager to continue their study of English and builds their pride in being able to speak accurately, fluently, and authentically.

Real language

Carefully exposing students to authentic, natural English, both receptively and productively, is a necessary component of building understanding and expression. All conversation models feature the language people really use; nowhere to be found is "textbook English" written merely to exemplify grammar.

Practical content

In addition to classic topical vocabulary, grammar, and conversation, *Top Notch* includes systematic practice of highly practical language, such as: how to advise someone on whether to take a bus or taxi, how to ask for foods at the table, how to compliment someone on their clothes, how to tell a friend about your weekend—usable language today's students want and need.

Memorable model conversations

Effective language instruction must make language memorable. The full range of social and functional communicative needs is presented through practical model conversations that are intensively practiced and manipulated, first within a guided model and then in freer and more personalized formats.

High-impact vocabulary syllabus

In order to ensure students' solid acquisition of vocabulary essential for communication, *Top Notch* contains explicit presentation, practice, and systematic extended recycling of words, collocations, and expressions appropriate at each level of study. The extensive captioned illustrations, photos, definitions, examples, and contextualized sentences remove doubts about meaning and provide a permanent in-book reference for student test preparation. An added benefit is that teachers don't have to search for pictures to bring to class and don't have to resort to translating vocabulary into the students' native language.

Learner-supportive grammar

Grammar is approached explicitly and cognitively, through form, meaning, and use. Charts provide examples and paradigms enhanced by simple usage notes at students' level of comprehension. This takes the guesswork out of meaning, makes lesson preparation easier for teachers, and provides students with comprehensible charts for permanent reference and test preparation. All presentations of grammar are followed by exercises to ensure adequate practice.

English as an international language

Top Notch prepares students for interaction with both native and non-native speakers of English, both linguistically and culturally. English is treated as an international language, rather than the language of a particular country or region. In addition, *Top Notch* helps students develop a cultural fluency by creating an awareness of the varied rules across cultures for: politeness, greetings and introductions, appropriateness of dress in different settings, conversation do's and taboos, table manners, and other similar issues.

Two beginning-level texts

Beginning students can be placed either in *Top Notch 1* or *Top Notch Fundamentals*, depending on ability and background. Even absolute beginners can start with confidence in *Top Notch Fundamentals*. False beginners can begin with *Top Notch 1*. The *Top Notch Placement Test* clarifies the best placement within the series.

Estimated teaching time

Each level of *Top Notch* is designed for 60 to 90 instructional hours and contains a full range of supplementary components and enrichment devices to tailor the course to individual needs.

Components of *Top Notch Fundamentals*

Student's Book

The Student's Book contains a bound-in Vocabulary Booster and Student's Take-Home Audio CD with pronunciation/intonation practice and the *Top Notch Pop* songs.

Teacher's Edition and Lesson Planner

Complete yet concise lesson plans are provided for each class. Corpus notes provide essential information from the *Longman Spoken American Corpus* and the *Longman Learner's Corpus*. In addition, a free Teacher's Resource Disk offers the following printable extension activities to personalize your teaching style:

- Grammar self-checks
- *Top Notch Pop* song activities
- Writing process worksheets
- Learning strategies
- Pronunciation activities and supplements
- Extra reading comprehension activities
- Vocabulary cards and cumulative vocabulary activities
- Graphic organizers
- Pair work cards

Copy & Go: Ready-made Interactive Activities for Busy Teachers

Interactive games, puzzles, and other practice activities in convenient photocopiable form support the Student's Book content and provide a welcome change of pace.

Complete Classroom Audio Program

The audio program contains listening comprehension activities, rhythm and intonation practice, and targeted pronunciation activities that focus on accurate and comprehensible pronunciation.

Because *Top Notch* prepares students for international communication, a variety of native and non-native speakers are included to ready students for the world outside the classroom. The audio program also includes the five *Top Notch Pop* songs in standard and karaoke form.

Workbook

A tightly linked illustrated Workbook contains exercises that provide additional practice and reinforcement of language concepts and skills from *Top Notch* and its Vocabulary Booster.

Complete Assessment Package with *ExamView®* Software

Fourteen easy-to-administer and easy-to-score unit achievement tests assess listening, vocabulary, grammar, social language, reading, and writing. Two review tests, one mid-book and one end-of-book, provide additional cumulative assessment. Two speaking tests assess progress in speaking. In addition to the photocopiable achievement tests, *ExamView®* software enables teachers to tailor-make tests to best meet their needs by combining items in any way they wish.

Top Notch TV

A lively and entertaining video offers a TV-style situation comedy that reintroduces language from each *Top Notch* unit, plus authentic unrehearsed interviews with English speakers from around the world and authentic karaoke. Packaged with the video are activity worksheets and a booklet with teaching suggestions and complete video scripts.

Companion Website

A Companion Website at www.longman.com/topnotch provides numerous additional resources for students and teachers. This no-cost, high-benefit feature includes opportunities for further practice of language and content from the *Top Notch* Student's Book.

Welcome to Top Notch!

About the Authors

Joan Saslow

Joan Saslow has taught English as a Foreign Language and English as a Second Language to adults and young adults in both South America and the United States. She taught English and French at the Binational Centers of Valparaíso and Viña del Mar, Chile, and the Catholic University of Valparaíso. Ms. Saslow taught English as a Foreign Language to Japanese university students at Marymount College and to international students in Westchester Community College's intensive English program as well as workplace English at the General Motors auto assembly plant in Tarrytown, NY.

Ms. Saslow is the series director of Longman's popular five-level adult series *True Colors: An EFL Course for Real Communication* and of *True Voices*, a five-level video course. She is author of *Ready to Go: Language, Lifeskills, and Civics*, a four-level adult ESL series; *Workplace Plus*, a vocational English series; and of *Literacy Plus*, a two-level series that teaches literacy, English, and culture to adult pre-literate students. She is also author of *English in Context: Reading Comprehension for Science and Technology*, a three-level series for English for special purposes. In addition, Ms. Saslow has been an author, an editor of language teaching materials, a teacher-trainer, and a frequent speaker at gatherings of EFL and ESL teachers for over thirty years.

Allen Ascher

Allen Ascher has been a teacher and teacher-trainer in both China and the United States, as well as an administrator and a publisher. Mr. Ascher specialized in teaching listening and speaking to students at the Beijing Second Foreign Language Institute, to hotel workers at a major international hotel in China, and to Japanese students from Chubu University studying English at Ohio University. In New York, Mr. Ascher taught students of all language backgrounds and abilities at the City University of New York and he trained teachers in the TESOL Certificate Program at the New School. He was also the academic director of the International English Language Institute at Hunter College.

Mr. Ascher has provided lively workshops for EFL teachers throughout Asia, Latin America, Europe, and the Middle East. He is author of the popular *Think about Editing: A Grammar Editing Guide for ESL Writers*. As a publisher, Mr. Ascher played a key role in the creation of some of the most widely used materials for adults, including: *True Colors, NorthStar, Focus on Grammar, Global Links*, and *Ready to Go*. Mr. Ascher has an MA in Applied Linguistics from Ohio University.

Welcome to Top Notch!

LESSON 1

Introduce Yourself

A 🎧 **MODEL. Read and listen.**

Martin: Hi. I'm Martin.
Ben: Hi, Martin. I'm Ben.

Martin: Nice to meet you, Ben.
Ben: Nice to meet you, too.

B 🎧 **Rhythm and intonation practice**

CONVERSATION

PAIR WORK. Now introduce yourself to your classmates.

🎧 **Greetings**
Hi.
Hello.
I'm [Lisa].

🎧 **Responses**
Nice to meet you.
Glad to meet you.
It's a pleasure to meet you.

2 ▶ Greet People

A 🎧 **MODEL.** Read and listen.

Yoko: Hi, Len. How are you?
Len: Fine, thanks. And you?
Yoko: I'm fine.

B 🎧 **Rhythm and intonation practice**

C 🎧 **VOCABULARY.** More greetings. Listen and practice.

1. Good morning. `8:00 A.M.`

2. Good afternoon. `2:00 P.M.`

3. Good evening. `6:00 P.M.`

CONVERSATION

PAIR WORK. Now greet your classmates.

🎧 **Greetings**
How are you?
How's everything?
How's it going?

🎧 **Responses**
Fine.
I'm fine.
Great.
Not bad.
So-so.

3 Say Good-bye

A 🎧 MODEL. Read and listen.

Emily: Good-bye, Charlotte.
Charlotte: Good-bye, Emily.
Emily: See you tomorrow.
Charlotte: OK. See you!

B 🎧 Rhythm and intonation practice

CONVERSATION

PAIR WORK. Now say good-bye to your classmates.

🎧 **Ways to say good-bye**
Good-bye.
Bye-bye.
Bye.
See you later.
See you tomorrow.
Take care.
Good night.

✔ *Now I can...*
☐ introduce myself.
☐ greet people.
☐ say good-bye.

Welcome to Top Notch! **3**

Names and Occupations

LESSON 1

Talk about What You Do

A 🎧 VOCABULARY. Occupations. Listen and practice.

1. a student

2. a teacher

3. an athlete

4. a writer

5. an actor

6. a pilot

7. a doctor

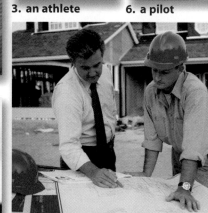
8. an engineer

9. an architect

10. a nurse

11. a flight attendant

12. a singer

📖 **VOCABULARY BOOSTER** See page V1 for more.

B 🎧 LISTENING COMPREHENSION. Listen for the vocabulary. Check ☑ the occupation you hear.

1. ☐ a nurse   ☑ an actor
2. ☐ a teacher   ☐ a writer
3. ☐ a doctor   ☐ an engineer

4. ☐ a student   ☐ a teacher
5. ☐ an architect   ☐ a singer

C GRAMMAR. Be: singular statements

Affirmative statements

I **am** Tony. / I**'m** Tony.

You **are** an engineer. / You**'re** an engineer.

He **is** a teacher. / He**'s** a teacher.

She **is** a nurse. / She**'s** a nurse.

Negative statements

I **am not** Tim. / I**'m not** Tim.

You **are not** an architect. / You**'re not** an architect.

He **is not** a student. / He**'s not** a student.

She **is not** a doctor. / She**'s not** a doctor.

Contractions
I am → I**'m**
He is → He**'s**
She is → She**'s**

Articles *a / an*
a teacher
an actor

D Write the article.

1. <u>an</u> architect   3. _____ writer   5. _____ nurse

2. _____ student   4. _____ engineer   6. _____ athlete

E Read the names and occupations. Then write about each person. Write affirmative and negative statements.

Denzel Washington
actor

Nora
singer

Se Ri Pak
athlete

Gabriel Garcia Marquez
writer

1. Denzel Washington ___He's an actor. He's not a singer.___

2. Nora _____ .

3. Se Ri Pak _____ .

4. Gabriel Garcia Marquez _____ .

CONVERSATION • *Talk about what you do.*

1. 🎧 **MODEL. Read and listen.**

Man: What do you do?

Woman: I'm an architect. And you?

Man: I'm a banker.

2. 🎧 **Rhythm and intonation practice**

3. PAIR WORK. Practice with your partner. Use real information. Use this guide:

A: What do you do?

B: I'm _____. And you?

A: I'm _____.

5

Identify People

A 🎧 VOCABULARY. More occupations. Listen and practice.

1. a chef

2. a manager

3. a banker

4. an artist

5. a musician

6. a scientist

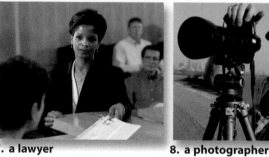
7. a lawyer

8. a photographer

B GRAMMAR. Singular and plural nouns / be: plural statements

Singular nouns	Plural nouns
a chef	2 chefs
an athlete	3 athletes

Contractions
We are → **We're**
You are → **You're**
They are → **They're**

Affirmative statements

We **are** lawyers. / We**'re** lawyers.

You **are** flight attendants. / You**'re** flight attendants.

They **are** musicians. / They**'re** musicians.

Negative statements

We **are not** chefs. / We**'re not** chefs.

You **are not** pilots. / You**'re not** pilots.

They **are not** writers. / They**'re not** writers.

Subject pronouns

Singular	Plural
I	we
you	you
he	they
she	

C Complete each statement with an occupation from the vocabulary on this page and page 4. Remember: Use <u>a</u> or <u>an</u> with singular nouns.

1. I am _____.

2. We are _____.

3. She is _____.

4. They are _____.

D Complete each statement with a form of <u>be</u>.

1. I _____ a writer.

2. She _____ not a pilot.

3. We _____ photographers.

4. They _____ not scientists.

Yes / no questions	Short answers
Are you Laura?	Yes, I am. / No, I'm not.
Is he a manager?	Yes, he is. / No, he's not.
Is Marie a teacher?	Yes, she is. / No, she's not.
Are you pilots?	Yes, we are. / No, we're not.
Are they musicians?	Yes, they are. / No, they're not.
Are they Ann and Bob?	Yes, they are. / No, they're not.

Be careful!
Yes, I am. NOT ~~Yes, I'm.~~
Yes, she is. NOT ~~Yes, she's.~~
Yes, we are. NOT ~~Yes, we're.~~

F Complete the questions and answers.

1. **A:** _Is_ she Joanne?

   B: No, _____ not. She'_____ Linda.

2. **A:** _____ a manager?

   B: Yes, I _____.

3. **A:** Is _____ Ted?

   B: _____, he'_____. He's John.

4. **A:** _____ they Fran and Al?

   B: Yes, _____.

5. **A:** _____ you Ellen and Herb?

   B: No, we'_____. _____ Peter and Diane.

CONVERSATION • *Identify a classmate.*

1. 🎧 **MODEL.** Read and listen.

Jake: Excuse me. Are you Marie?
Laura: No, I'm not. I'm Laura. That's Marie.
Jake: Where?
Laura: Right over there.
Jake: Thank you.
Laura: You're welcome.

2. 🎧 **Rhythm and intonation practice**

3. **PAIR WORK.** Practice the conversation.
Use your <u>own</u> names in the guide.

A: Excuse me. Are you _____?
B: No, I'm not. I'm _____. That's _____.
A: Where?
B: Right over there.
A: Thank you.
B: You're welcome.

LESSON 3

Spell Names

A 🎧 **VOCABULARY.** The alphabet. Listen and practice.

ABCDEFGHIJKLM
NOPQRSTUVWXYZ

B 🎧 **LISTENING COMPREHENSION.** Listen. Circle the letter you hear.

1. M D	4. R S	7. T C	10. I U
2. P V	5. B Z	8. D B	11. E I
3. B K	6. F X	9. E A	12. R O

C **PAIR WORK.** Read the letters aloud to your partner. Point to the letters you hear.

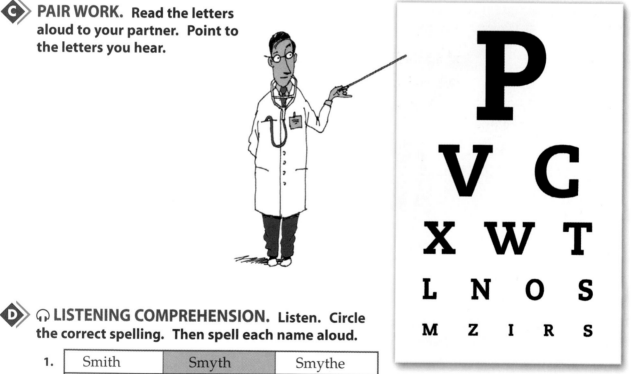

D 🎧 **LISTENING COMPREHENSION.** Listen. Circle the correct spelling. Then spell each name aloud.

1.	Smith	Smyth	Smythe
2.	Karen	Caren	Caryn
3.	Bill Gates	Gil Bates	Phil Tates

E 🎧 **LISTENING COMPREHENSION.** Listen to the conversations. Write the names.

1. _____ 2. _____ 3. _____

F. GRAMMAR. Proper nouns and common nouns

Proper nouns

The names of people and places are proper nouns. Use a capital letter to begin a proper noun.

    Irene Linden   New York   Mexico City

Common nouns

Other nouns are common nouns. Use a lowercase letter to begin a common noun.

    doctor   architect   student   man

G. WHAT ABOUT YOU? Write proper and common nouns. Use a capital letter for proper nouns.

Proper nouns

1. Your teacher's name: _____

2. Your name: _____

Common nouns

3. Your occupation: _____

4. A partner's occupation: _____

H. PRONUNCIATION. Syllables. Listen and practice.

1 syllable	2 syllables	3 syllables	4 syllables
chef	bank•er	ar•chi•tect	pho•tog•ra•pher

Now listen and write the number of syllables.

1. nurse _____

2. nurses _____

3. teacher _____

4. assistant _____

5. scientist _____

6. musician _____

CONVERSATION • *Spell a name.*

1. MODEL. Read and listen.

Mr. Bello: Hello. I'm John Bello.

Ms. Quinn: Excuse me?

Mr. Bello: John Bello.

Ms. Quinn: How do you spell that?

Mr. Bello: B-E-L-L-O.

2. Rhythm and intonation practice

3. PAIR WORK. Practice the conversation. Use your <u>own</u> name in the guide.

A: Hello. I'm _____.

B: Excuse me?

A: _____.

B: How do you spell that?

A: _____.

TOP NOTCH
ACTIVITIES

A 🎧 **LISTENING COMPREHENSION.** Listen. Then check ☑ the occupation you hear.

1. ☐

☐

2. ☐

☐

3. ☐

☐

B 🎧 **LISTENING COMPREHENSION.** Listen. Then listen again and complete the information.

Available for charters

John _____

PILOT

Licensed
Insured   john@airtaxi.com

**World Language
Institute**

Lorraine Clare   1-800-555-6788

English _____

NAME:	*Porter*
OCCUPATION:	

C **WHAT ABOUT YOU?**
Complete the form. Use
your <u>own</u> information.

NAME	OCCUPATION

D **WRITING.** Answer in your <u>own</u> way.

1. "Hi. I'm Iris Glass."

   YOU _____.

2. "Nice to meet you."

   YOU _____.

3. "Are you a teacher?"

   YOU _____.

4. "What do you do?"

   YOU _____.

5. "Thank you."

   YOU _____.

6. "Good-bye."

   YOU _____.

E **SPELLING BEE.** Form teams. Say and spell occupations.

nurses

Team A   N-U-R-S-E-S

TOP NOTCH WEBSITE
For Unit 1 online activities, visit the
Top Notch Companion Website at
www.longman.com/topnotch.

- **Vocabulary.** Point and name the occupations of the people.
  She's a pilot. They're flight attendants.

- **Grammar.** Ask and answer questions about the people.
  A: Is she a doctor?
  B: Yes, she is.

- **Social language.** Create conversations for the people.
  A: Hello. I'm _____.
  B: Nice to meet you.

✔ **Now I can...**

☐ talk about what I do.
☐ identify people.
☐ spell names.

UNIT 2

Relationships

UNIT GOALS

1 Introduce people
2 Tell someone your first and last name
3 Get someone's address and phone number

1 Introduce People

A GRAMMAR. Possessive adjectives and nouns

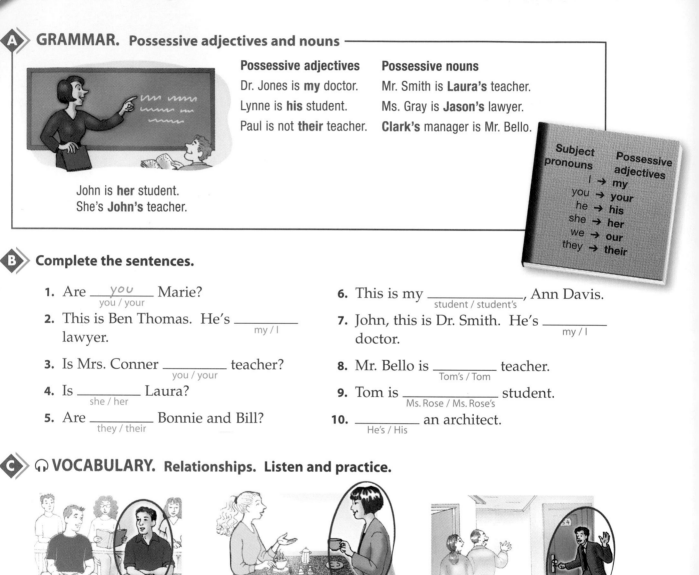

Possessive adjectives
Dr. Jones is **my** doctor.
Lynne is **his** student.
Paul is not **their** teacher.

Possessive nouns
Mr. Smith is **Laura's** teacher.
Ms. Gray is **Jason's** lawyer.
Clark's manager is Mr. Bello.

John is **her** student.
She's **John's** teacher.

Subject pronouns		Possessive adjectives
I	→	my
you	→	your
he	→	his
she	→	her
we	→	our
they	→	their

B Complete the sentences.

1. Are ___*you*___ Marie?
   <small>you / your</small>

2. This is Ben Thomas. He's _____ lawyer.
   <small>my / I</small>

3. Is Mrs. Conner _____ teacher?
   <small>you / your</small>

4. Is _____ Laura?
   <small>she / her</small>

5. Are _____ Bonnie and Bill?
   <small>they / their</small>

6. This is my _____, Ann Davis.
   <small>student / student's</small>

7. John, this is Dr. Smith. He's _____ doctor.
   <small>my / I</small>

8. Mr. Bello is _____ teacher.
   <small>Tom's / Tom</small>

9. Tom is _____ student.
   <small>Ms. Rose / Ms. Rose's</small>

10. _____ an architect.
    <small>He's / His</small>

C ⌂ VOCABULARY. Relationships. Listen and practice.

1. a classmate   2. a friend   3. a neighbor

4. a boss   5. a colleague

VOCABULARY BOOSTER See page V1 for more.

D 🎧 **LISTENING COMPREHENSION.** **Listen.** **Complete the sentences with the relationship vocabulary.**

1. Ben is her _classmate_.

2. Tania is his _____.

3. Ms. Quinn is her _____.

4. Larry is his _____.

5. Ann is his _____.

CONVERSATION • *Introduce people.*

1. 🎧 **MODEL.** **Read and listen.**

David: Tom, this is Paula. Paula's my classmate.

Tom: Hi, Paula.

Paula: Hi, Tom. Nice to meet you.

Tom: Nice to meet you, too.

2. 🎧 **Rhythm and intonation practice**

3. **GROUP WORK.** **Introduce classmates in your class. Use the guide.**

A: _____, this is _____.
_____'s my _____.

B: Hi, _____.

C: Hi, _____. Nice to meet you.

B: Nice to meet you, too.

13

Tell Someone Your First and Last Name

A 🎧 **VOCABULARY.** Titles and names. Listen and practice.

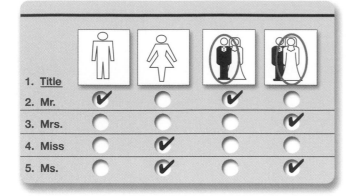

1. Title				
2. Mr.	✔	○	✔	○
3. Mrs.	○	○	○	✔
4. Miss	○	✔	○	○
5. Ms.	○	✔	○	✔

Mr. Charles Lee   Mrs. Vivian Lee

6. first name   7. last name

📖 **VOCABULARY BOOSTER** See page V1 for more.

Be careful!
Mr. Charles Lee OR Mr. Lee
NOT ~~Mr. Charles~~

B 🎧 **LISTENING COMPREHENSION.** Listen to the questions about first and last names. Circle the names.

1.

☒ Mr.
☐ Mrs.   Hugo Silva
☐ Miss
☐ Ms.

2.

☐ Mr.
☐ Mrs.   Ruth Barnes
☐ Miss
☒ Ms.

3.

☒ Mr.
☐ Mrs.   Tom Wong
☐ Miss
☐ Ms.

4.

☐ Mr.
☐ Mrs.   Ann Stone
☐ Miss
☒ Ms.

5.

☐ Mr.
☒ Mrs.   Wendy Roberts
☐ Miss
☐ Ms.

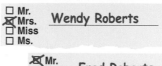
☒ Mr.
☐ Mrs.   Fred Roberts
☐ Miss
☐ Ms.

6.

☐ Mr.
☐ Mrs.   Pam Garcia
☐ Miss
☒ Ms.

☒ Mr.
☐ Mrs.   Henry Solas
☐ Miss
☐ Ms.

C ▸ **WHAT ABOUT YOU?** Fill out the form with <u>your</u> name. Check ☑ your title.

☐ Mr.
☐ Mrs.
☐ Miss   _____ _____
☐ Ms.   *first name*   *last name*

CONVERSATION • *Tell someone your first and last name.*

1. 🎧 **MODEL.** Read and listen.

Clerk: What's your last name, please?

Mr. Fava: Fava.

Clerk: And your first name?

Mr. Fava: My first name? Bob.

Clerk: Thank you, Mr. Fava.

Mr. Fava: You're welcome.

2. 🎧 **Rhythm and intonation practice**

3. **PAIR WORK.** Practice the conversation with your <u>own</u> name. Write your partner's information.

A: What's your last name, please?

B: _____.

A: And your first name?

B: _____.

A: Thank you, _____.

B: You're welcome.

_____ _____
first name   *last name*

Get Someone's Address and Phone Number

A 🎧 VOCABULARY. Numbers 0–20. Listen and practice.

0 zero	7 seven	14 fourteen
1 one	8 eight	15 fifteen
2 two	9 nine	16 sixteen
3 three	10 ten	17 seventeen
4 four	11 eleven	18 eighteen
5 five	12 twelve	19 nineteen
6 six	13 thirteen	20 twenty

B PAIR WORK. Listen while your partner reads a number. Write the number on a separate piece of paper.

EXPENSE REPORT NO. 0248204927

VISTA
JORGE SILVA
5600 3490 2283 0098

Passport No.
368709828

ISBN 0-399-14446-3

C 🎧 LISTENING COMPREHENSION. Listen. Write the phone numbers. Then listen again to check your work.

Name	Telephone number
1. Barbara Jackson	___ - ___
2. John Nack	___ - ___ - ___
3. Mike Quinn	___ - ___
4. Judy Opper	___ - ___ - ___ - ___

D GRAMMAR. Be: information questions with What

Questions	Answers
What's her last name?	Hayek.
What's her phone number?	57-34-0078.
What's his first name?	George.
What's his e-mail address?	Benson@allnet.com.
What's their address?	14 Bolivar Street, Maracaibo, Venezuela.

What is → What's

In phone numbers, say oh for zero:
0078 = oh-oh-seven-eight.

In e-mail addresses, say benson **at** allnet **dot** com.

E Complete the questions.

1. **A:** ___What's his___ address?
   B: 11 Main Street.

2. **A:** _____ phone number?
   B: 22-63-140.

3. **A:** _____ address?
   B: 18 Bank Street.

4. **A:** _____ cell-phone number?
   B: 878-456-0055.

5. **A:** _____ e-mail address?
   B: sgast@mp.net.

6. **A:** _____ phone number?
   B: 44-78-35.

F 🎧 **PRONUNCIATION.** Stress in two-word pairs. Listen and practice.

• •
first name

• •
last name

• • •
phone num ber

• • •
e mail ad dress

CONVERSATION • *Get your partner's address, e-mail address, or phone number.*

1. 🎧 **MODEL.** Read and listen.

    Woman: What's your phone number?
    Man: 523-6620.
    Woman: 523-6620?
    Man: That's right.

2. 🎧 **Rhythm and intonation practice**

3. **PAIR WORK.** Practice the conversation. Write your partner's information on a piece of paper. Use this guide.

    A: What's your _____?
    B: _____.
    A: _____?
    B: That's right.

🎵 **TOP NOTCH SONG**
"Excuse Me, Please"
Lyrics on last book page.

A 🎧 **READING.** Read and listen. Where are they from?

TOP NOTCH WEBSITE
For Unit 2 online activities, visit the
Top Notch Companion Website at
www.longman.com/topnotch.

Famous People around the World

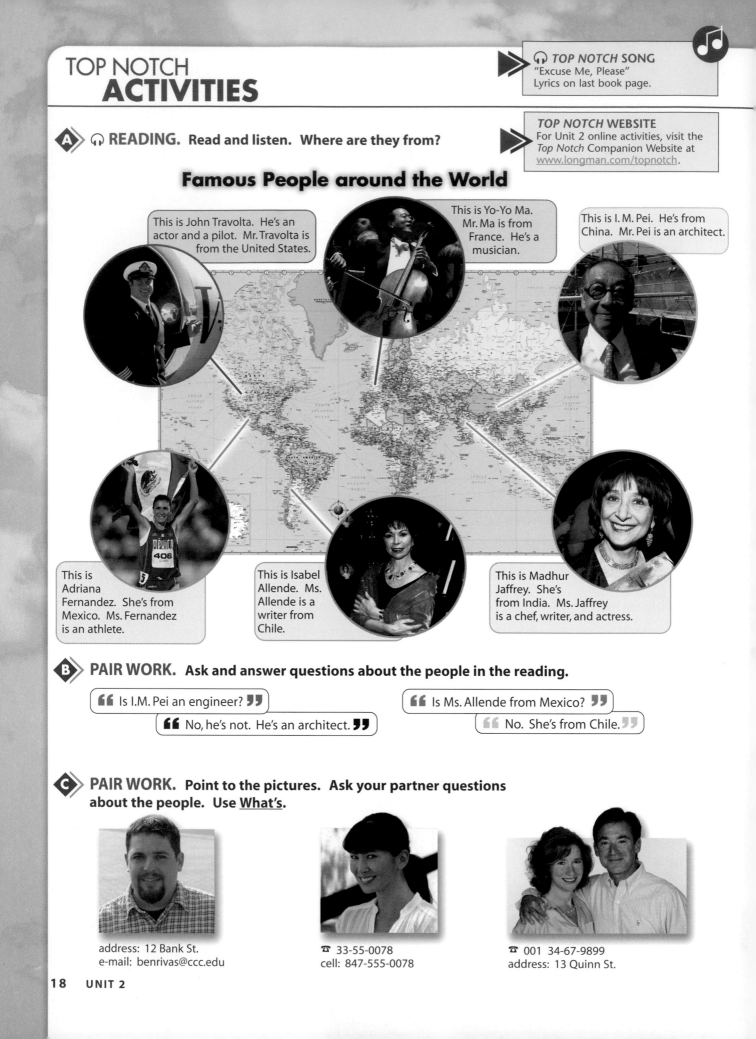

This is John Travolta. He's an actor and a pilot. Mr. Travolta is from the United States.

This is Yo-Yo Ma. Mr. Ma is from France. He's a musician.

This is I. M. Pei. He's from China. Mr. Pei is an architect.

This is Adriana Fernandez. She's from Mexico. Ms. Fernandez is an athlete.

This is Isabel Allende. Ms. Allende is a writer from Chile.

This is Madhur Jaffrey. She's from India. Ms. Jaffrey is a chef, writer, and actress.

B **PAIR WORK.** Ask and answer questions about the people in the reading.

❝ Is I.M. Pei an engineer? ❞

❝ No, he's not. He's an architect. ❞

❝ Is Ms. Allende from Mexico? ❞

❝ No. She's from Chile. ❞

C **PAIR WORK.** Point to the pictures. Ask your partner questions about the people. Use <u>What's</u>.

address: 12 Bank St.
e-mail: benrivas@ccc.edu

☎ 33-55-0078
cell: 847-555-0078

☎ 001 34-67-9899
address: 13 Quinn St.

Unit Wrap-Up

- **Vocabulary.** Point and name the relationships.
  Boss, friend, colleague . . .
- **Grammar.** Write sentences about the picture.
  She's his colleague.
- **Social language.** Create conversations for the people.
  A: What's your last name?
  B: _____.

First name: _____ Last name: _____
Phone: _____
E-mail address: _____
Address: _____

High St. Main St.

14

16

Allie Cruz
Bank Manager

Now I can . . .

☐ introduce people.
☐ tell someone my first and last name.
☐ get someone's address and phone number.

Directions and Transportation

UNIT GOALS

1 Ask about the location of places
2 Give and get directions
3 Suggest a means of transportation

LESSON 1

Ask about the Location of Places

A 🎧 **VOCABULARY.** Places in the community. Listen and practice.

1. a pharmacy

2. a restaurant

3. a post office

4. a travel agency

5. a bank

6. a newsstand

7. a convenience store

8. a bookstore

📖 **VOCABULARY BOOSTER** See page V2 for more.

B 🎧 **LISTENING COMPREHENSION.**
Listen. Number the places.

_____ a bookstore

_____ a travel agency

___1___ a newsstand

_____ a bank

_____ a pharmacy

C 🎧 **VOCABULARY.** Locations and directions.
Listen and practice.

1. across the street

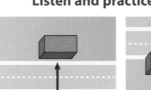
2. around the corner

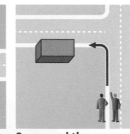
3. down the street

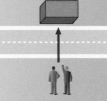
4. on the left

5. on the right

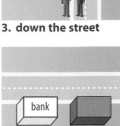
6. next to the bank

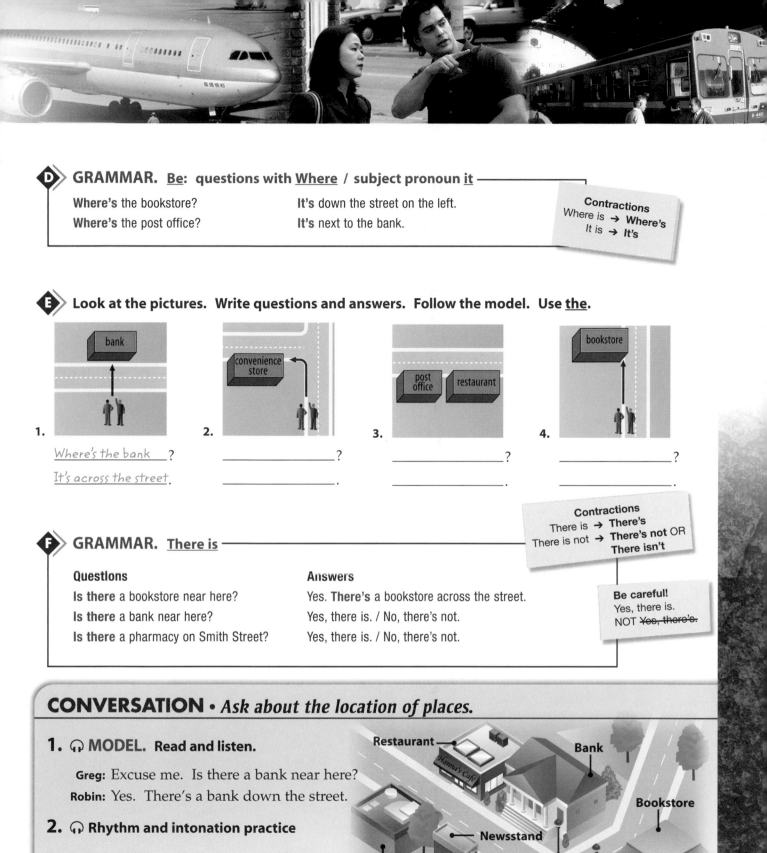

D GRAMMAR. Be: questions with Where / subject pronoun it

Where's the bookstore?   **It's** down the street on the left.
Where's the post office?   **It's** next to the bank.

Contractions
Where is → **Where's**
It is → **It's**

E Look at the pictures. Write questions and answers. Follow the model. Use the.

1.
Where's the bank ?
It's across the street.

2.
_____ ?
_____ .

3.
_____ ?
_____ .

4.
_____ ?
_____ .

F GRAMMAR. There is

Contractions
There is → **There's**
There is not → **There's not** OR
There isn't

Be careful!
Yes, there is.
NOT ~~Yes, there's.~~

Questions	Answers
Is there a bookstore near here?	Yes. **There's** a bookstore across the street.
Is there a bank near here?	Yes, there is. / No, there's not.
Is there a pharmacy on Smith Street?	Yes, there is. / No, there's not.

CONVERSATION • Ask about the location of places.

1. 🎧 **MODEL. Read and listen.**

Greg: Excuse me. Is there a bank near here?
Robin: Yes. There's a bank down the street.

2. 🎧 **Rhythm and intonation practice**

3. PAIR WORK. Practice the conversation with the map and this guide.

A: Excuse me. Is there _____ near here?
B: Yes. There's a _____.

Continue with more questions and answers.

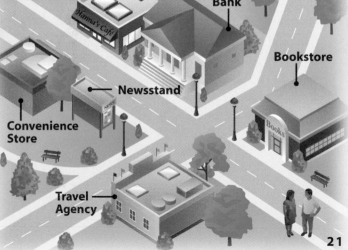

21

Give and Get Directions

A 🎧 **VOCABULARY.** More places in the community. **Listen and practice.**

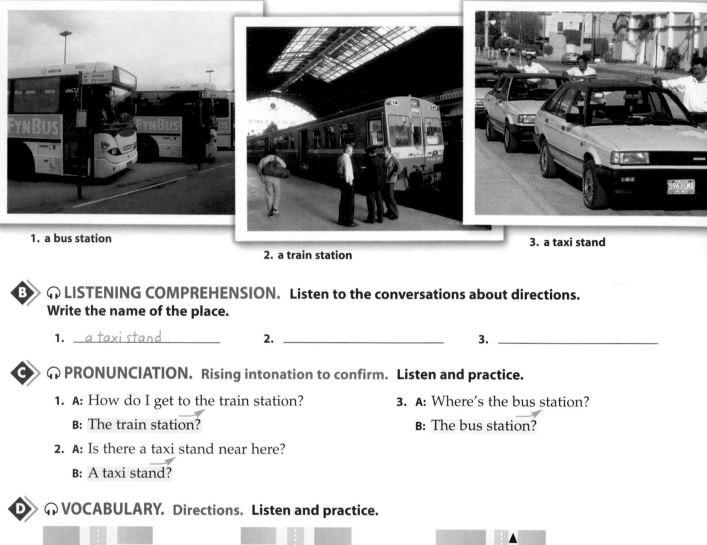

1. a bus station

2. a train station

3. a taxi stand

B 🎧 **LISTENING COMPREHENSION.** **Listen to the conversations about directions. Write the name of the place.**

1. _a taxi stand_   2. _____   3. _____

C 🎧 **PRONUNCIATION.** Rising intonation to confirm. **Listen and practice.**

1. **A:** How do I get to the train station?

   B: The train station?

2. **A:** Is there a taxi stand near here?

   B: A taxi stand?

3. **A:** Where's the bus station?

   B: The bus station?

D 🎧 **VOCABULARY.** Directions. **Listen and practice.**

1. Turn right.
   OR: Turn right at the corner.

2. Turn left.
   OR: Turn left at the corner.

3. Go straight.

4. Go to the corner of Main Street and Park Avenue.

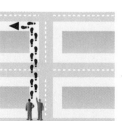

5. Go two blocks and turn left.

Write directions to match the pictures.

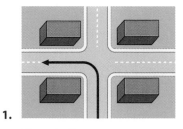

1.
<u>Turn left at the corner</u>.

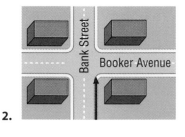

2.
_____ .

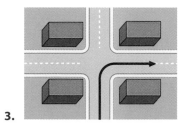

3.
_____ .

4.
_____ .

CONVERSATION • *Give and get directions.*

1. 🎧 **MODEL. Read and listen.**

Felix: Excuse me. How do I get to the train station?

Susan: The train station? Go one block and turn right.

Felix: Thanks!

Susan: No problem.

2. 🎧 **Rhythm and intonation practice**

3. PAIR WORK. Practice the conversation with the map and this guide.

A: Excuse me. How do I get to the _____?

B: The _____? _____.

A: Thanks!

B: _____.

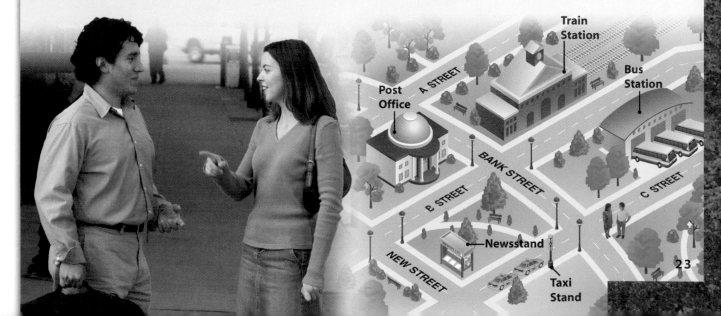

23

3 *Suggest a Means of Transportation*

A ⌕ VOCABULARY. More places. Listen and practice.

1. a stadium

2. a park

3. a mall

4. a museum

5. an airport

B PAIR WORK. Look at the map. Ask and answer questions. Use the vocabulary.

❝ Where's the stadium? ❞

❝ It's next to the mall. ❞

Bus Station

Central Train Station

Park City Museum

D STREET

CENTRAL AVENUE

Park

City Mall

SMITH STREET

Airport

Smith Street Stadium

C GRAMMAR. The imperative

Take the train to the museum.   Don't take the bus.

Use imperatives to give directions.

Affirmative

Take a taxi.   Drive.   Walk.

Negative

Don't take a taxi.   Don't drive.   Don't walk.

LESSON

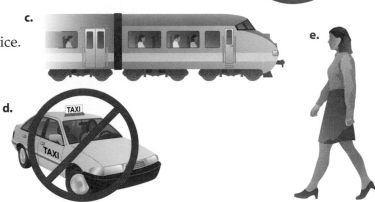

D **Match each sentence with a picture.**

1. __e__ Walk to the mall.

2. _____ Don't take the bus to the post office.

3. _____ Take the train to the stadium.

4. _____ Don't drive to the park.

5. _____ Don't take a taxi to the airport.

CONVERSATION • *Suggest a means of transportation.*

1. ⌒ MODEL. Read and listen.

Fumiyo: How do I get to the Metropolitan Museum?

Jeff: Don't walk. Take the bus.

Fumiyo: The bus?

Jeff: Yes, that's right.

Fumiyo: Thanks.

Jeff: You're welcome.

2. ⌒ Rhythm and intonation practice

3. Make a list of places in <u>your</u> city or town.

4. PAIR WORK. Now practice the conversation with your list and this guide.

A: How do I get to _____?

B: Don't _____. _____.

A: _____?

B: Yes, that's right.

A: _____.

B: _____.

25

TOP NOTCH
ACTIVITIES

TOP NOTCH **WEBSITE**
For Unit 3 online activities, visit the
Top Notch Companion Website at
www.longman.com/topnotch.

A ⌒ **READING.** Read and listen. Is there a museum in your city?

GUIDE TO THE **WORLD'S GREAT MUSEUMS**

National Palace Museum, Taipei

The National Palace Museum is on Chih-shan Road in the Wai-shuang-hsi district of Taipei.

Transportation: Take bus 213, 255, or 304, or take a taxi.

The National Museum of Anthropology is in Mexico City. It is in Chapultepec Park, section 1.

Transportation: Take a taxi or take the number 7 train to Auditorio metro station.

National Museum of Anthropology, Mexico City

MUSEO NACIONAL DE ANTROPOLOGÍA

Kyoto National Museum, Kyoto

The Kyoto National Museum is at 527 Chayamachi, Higashiyama-ku.

Transportation: Take the Japan Rail train to Kyoto Station. Then bus 206 or 208. Walk from the bus stop to the museum.

B Read about the museums again. Write answers to the questions.

1. Is there a train to the National Museum of Anthropology? _____ .
2. Where is the National Palace Museum? _____ .
3. How do I get to the Kyoto National Museum? _____ .

C **PAIR WORK.** Make a map of a neighborhood in your town. Write the names of the streets and places. Then practice giving and getting directions to places on your map.

NEED HELP? **Here's language you already know:**

Discuss locations	Give advice	Give directions	Respond
Excuse me.	Take [the train].	Turn [right] at the corner.	Thanks.
How do I get to the [train station]?	Walk.	Turn [left].	You're welcome.
Where's the [bus station]?	Drive.	Go straight.	No problem.
Is there a [bank] near here?	Don't [take the bus].	Go to the corner of [First Street] and [Main Street].	
Yes, there is. / No, there isn't.		Go [two] blocks and turn [right].	
There's a [bank] [around the corner].			
It's [across the street].			

UNIT WRAP-UP

- **Vocabulary.** Name the places in the town.
  A restaurant, a newsstand . . .

- **Grammar.** Make statements about location.
  The restaurant is across from the bus station.

- **Social language.** Ask for directions.
  A: Where's the mall?
  B: It's around the corner, on the left.

City Mall

Central Train Station

UniBank

ATM

Second Street
Books

THE PARK MUSEUM

Taxi

Post Office

Second Street

PARADISE TRAVEL

Mason Street

South Side
Bus Station

Oak Street

GET IT HERE
Convenience Store

First Street

✔ **Now I can . . .**

☐ ask about the location
  of places.
☐ give and get directions.
☐ suggest a means of
  transportation.

27

People

UNIT GOALS

1 Identify family members
2 Talk about your family
3 Describe people

LESSON 1

Identify Family Members

A 🎧 **VOCABULARY.** Family members. Listen and practice.

1. grandparents

2. grandmother   3. grandfather

10. grandchildren

11. grandson   12. granddaughter

4. parents

5. mother   6. father

13. wife   14. husband

7. children

8. daughter   9. son

15. sister   16. brother

B 🎧 **LISTENING COMPREHENSION.** Listen to the woman talk about pictures of her family. Check ☑ the correct picture.

1. ☐ ☐   2. ☐ ☐   3. ☐ ☐

4. ☐ ☐   5. ☐ ☐   6. ☐ ☐

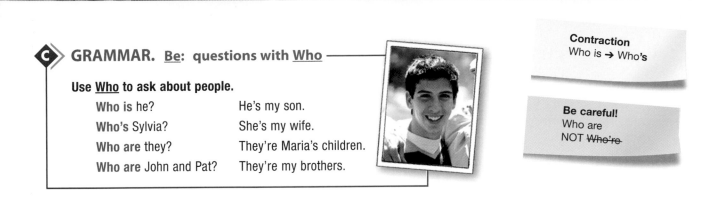

 GRAMMAR. **Be:** questions with **Who**

Use **Who** to ask about people.

Who is he?	He's my son.
Who's Sylvia?	She's my wife.
Who are they?	They're Maria's children.
Who are John and Pat?	They're my brothers.

> **Contraction**
> Who is → Who's

> **Be careful!**
> Who are
> NOT ~~Who're~~

D Write questions. Use **Who** and **he**, **she**, or **they**.

1. **A:** _Who's she_ ?
   B: She's my grandmother.

2. **A:** _____ ?
   B: He's my father.

3. **A:** _____ ?
   B: She's Mrs. Finn's granddaughter.

4. **A:** _____ ?
   B: They're Peter's parents.

5. **A:** _____ ?
   B: He's Julie's husband.

6. **A:** _____ ?
   B: They're my brothers and sisters.

CONVERSATION • *Identify family members.*

1. **MODEL.** **Read and listen.**

   Bill: Who's that?
   Nancy: That's my father.
   Bill: And who are they?
   Nancy: They're my sisters, Julie and Trish.

2. **Rhythm and intonation practice**

3. **PAIR WORK.** **Bring in family photos, or write the names of the people in your family. Then practice the conversation with this guide.**

   A: Who's _____?
   B: That's _____.
   B: And _____?
   B: _____.

Talk about Your Family

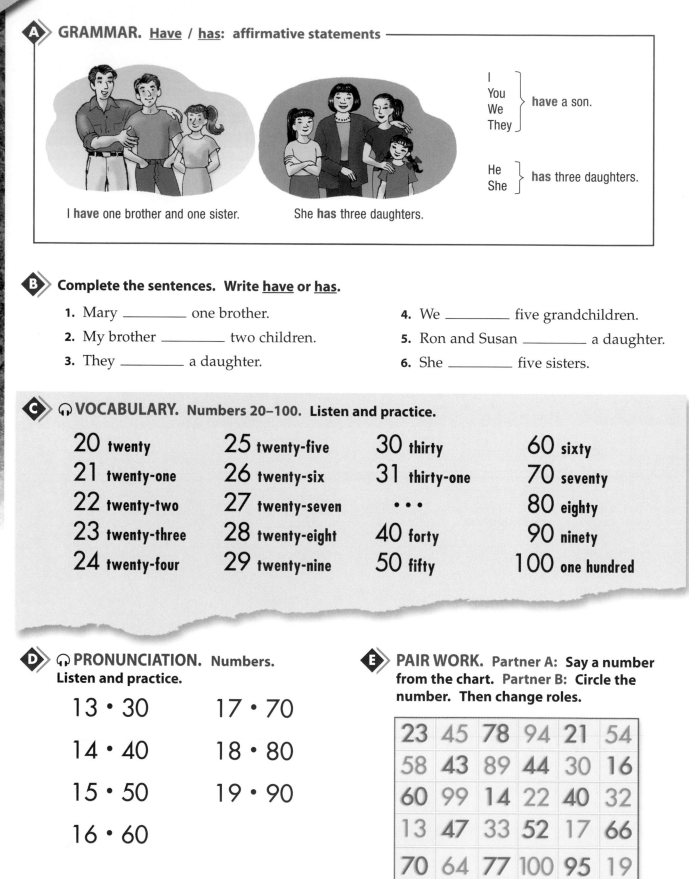

A ▷ **GRAMMAR.** Have / has: affirmative statements

I have one brother and one sister.

She has three daughters.

I / You / We / They **have** a son.

He / She **has** three daughters.

B ▷ Complete the sentences. Write **have** or **has**.

1. Mary _____ one brother.

2. My brother _____ two children.

3. They _____ a daughter.

4. We _____ five grandchildren.

5. Ron and Susan _____ a daughter.

6. She _____ five sisters.

C ▷ 🎧 **VOCABULARY.** Numbers 20–100. Listen and practice.

20 twenty	25 twenty-five	30 thirty	60 sixty
21 twenty-one	26 twenty-six	31 thirty-one	70 seventy
22 twenty-two	27 twenty-seven	• • •	80 eighty
23 twenty-three	28 twenty-eight	40 forty	90 ninety
24 twenty-four	29 twenty-nine	50 fifty	100 one hundred

D ▷ 🎧 **PRONUNCIATION.** Numbers. Listen and practice.

13 • 30   17 • 70

14 • 40   18 • 80

15 • 50   19 • 90

16 • 60

E ▷ **PAIR WORK.** Partner A: Say a number from the chart. Partner B: Circle the number. Then change roles.

23	45	78	94	21	54
58	43	89	44	30	16
60	99	14	22	40	32
13	47	33	52	17	66
70	64	77	100	95	19

GRAMMAR. <u>Be</u>: questions with <u>How old</u>

How old is he?	He's nineteen years old.
How old is your sister?	She's twenty.
How old is Kate?	Twenty-six.
How old are they?	He's thirty-six and she's twenty-eight.
How old are your grandparents?	They're both 84.

G Complete the questions with <u>How old is</u> or <u>How old are</u>.

1. <u>How old is</u> your brother?

2. _____ Matt's children?

3. _____ their grandparents?

4. _____ Helen's husband?

5. _____ his parents?

6. _____ her son?

CONVERSATION • *Talk about your family.*

1. 🎧 **MODEL. Read and listen.**

Ray: I have one brother and two sisters.

Tessa: Really? How old is your brother?

Ray: Twenty.

Tessa: And your sisters?

Ray: Eighteen and twenty-two.

2. 🎧 **Rhythm and intonation practice**

3. PAIR WORK. Talk about your <u>own</u> family. Start with the guide.

B: I have _____.

A: Really? How old _____?

B: _____ . . .

Continue the conversation about other people in your family.

NEED HELP? **Here's language you already know:**

And your [mother]?
What's his / her name?
What does he / she do?

31

3 Describe People

A ⌒ VOCABULARY. Adjectives to describe people. Listen and practice.

1. pretty

2. handsome

3. good-looking

4. cute

5. tall   6. short

7. old

8. young

📖 VOCABULARY BOOSTER See page V2 for more.

B GRAMMAR. Adjectives / very and so

Describe people with a form of be and an adjective.

She's **pretty**.	They're **tall**.
He's **handsome**.	Your children **are cute**.

The adverbs so and very make adjectives stronger.

His daughter is **so** cute!   She's **very** tall.

C ⌒ LISTENING COMPREHENSION. Listen to people describe their family members. Check ☑ the adjective.

	good-looking	pretty	cute	tall	short	young
1. Her husband is	☐	☐	☐	☐	☐	☐
2. His daughter is	☐	☐	☐	☐	☐	☐
3. Her brother is	☐	☐	☐	☐	☐	☐
4. His son is	☐	☐	☐	☐	☐	☐
5. Her father is	☐	☐	☐	☐	☐	☐
6. His sisters are	☐	☐	☐	☐	☐	☐

D Look at the pictures. Complete each sentence with a form of be and an adjective.

1. Your friends _are_ so _pretty_.   **2.** They _____ so _____.   **3.** His sister _____ very _____.

4. He ____ so ____.

5. His wife ____ so ____!

6. My grandparents ____ very ____.

CONVERSATION • *Describe people.*

1. 🎧 **MODEL.** **Read and listen.**

Eric: Tell me about your father.

Grace: Well, he's a doctor. He's very tall.

Eric: And how about your mother?

Grace: She's a lawyer. She's short, and she's very pretty.

2. 🎧 **Rhythm and intonation practice**

3. **PAIR WORK.** Describe people in <u>your</u> family. Use the guide, or create a new conversation.

A: Tell me about your ____.

B: ____.

A: And how about your ____?

B: ____.

33

♫ **TOP NOTCH SONG**
"Tell Me All about It"
Lyrics on last book page.

TOP NOTCH WEBSITE
For Unit 4 online activities, visit the
Top Notch Companion Website at
www.longman.com/topnotch.

A ♫ **READING.** Read and listen.

Who are they?

This is Jackie Chan. Jackie Chan is a movie star and singer from Hong Kong. His wife, Joan Lin, is an actress from Taiwan. They have a son, JC Chan. He's a student in the United States.

Meet Venus and Serena Williams. Venus and her sister are famous tennis players. Their mother's name is Oracene Price. Their father, Richard Williams, is their manager. Venus and Serena have two more sisters—Isha and Lyndrea. But they're not tennis players.

Meet Alejandro Fernandez and his father, Vicente. They're from Mexico. They are both singers, and they are famous all over Latin America. Vicente and his wife, Maria del Refugio Abarca, have three sons in all—Alejandro and his two brothers, Gerardo and Vicente Jr.

B **Read about the people again. Complete the sentences.**

1. Jackie Chan is JC Chan's _father_.
2. _____ is Joan Lin's husband.
3. Isha Williams is Venus and Serena's _____.
4. _____ Williams is Venus and Serena Williams's manager.
5. Maria del Refugio Abarca is Alejandro's _____.
6. Gerardo Fernandez is Vicente Jr.'s _____.

C **PAIR WORK.** Interview your partner about his or her family.

NEED HELP? **Here's language you already know:**

Tell me about your family.	What does your [sister] do?
How old is your [mother]?	Is your [brother] [good-looking]?
What's your [mother]'s occupation?	Are your [sister]s [tall]?

I have [two] [children].
My [husband] is [short].
My [brothers] are very [tall].
My [sister] is a [student].

D **WRITING.** On a separate piece of paper, write about your partner's family.

UNIT WRAP-UP

- **Vocabulary.** Describe the people.
  He's very good-looking.
  She's tall.

- **Grammar.** Make statements about the families. Use <u>have</u> or <u>has</u>.
  They have two grandchildren.

- **Social language.** Point to family members and talk about the relationships.
  A: Who's she?
  B: She's his wife.

✔	*Now I can …*
☐	identify my family members.
☐	talk about my family.
☐	describe people.

35

Events and Times

UNIT GOALS

1 Talk about time
2 Invite someone to an event
3 Talk about dates

LESSON 1

Talk about Time

A 🎧 **VOCABULARY.** What time is it? Listen and practice.

1. It's one o'clock.

2. It's one fifteen.
  It's a quarter after one.

3. It's one twenty.
  It's twenty after one.

4. It's one thirty.
  It's half past one.

5. It's one forty.
  It's twenty to two.

6. It's one forty-five.
  It's a quarter to two.

7. It's noon.

8. It's midnight.

24:00 → 11:59 = A.M.
12:00 → 23:59 = P.M.

Say *eight* A.M. or *eight* P.M.

B **PAIR WORK.** It's noon in London. Ask your partner about times in cities around the world.

❝ What time is it in Cairo? ❞

  ❝ It's 2:00 P.M. ❞

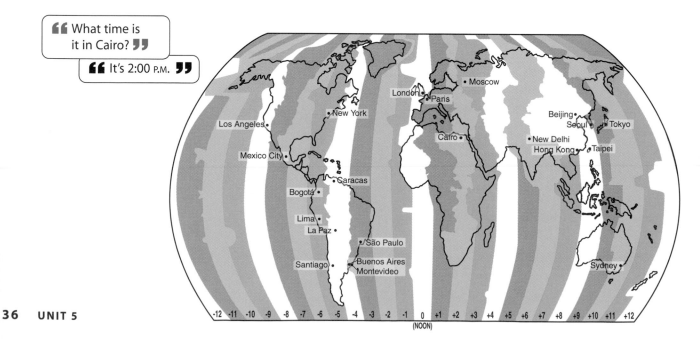

C 🎧 **PRONUNCIATION.** Sentence stress. **Listen and practice.**

1. It's a **quar**ter to **two**.

2. It's **twen**ty to **one**.

3. It's **ten** after **five**.

D 🎧 **VOCABULARY.** <u>Early</u>, <u>on time</u>, and <u>late</u>. **Listen and practice.**

1. early

2. on time

3. late

CONVERSATION • *Talk about time.*

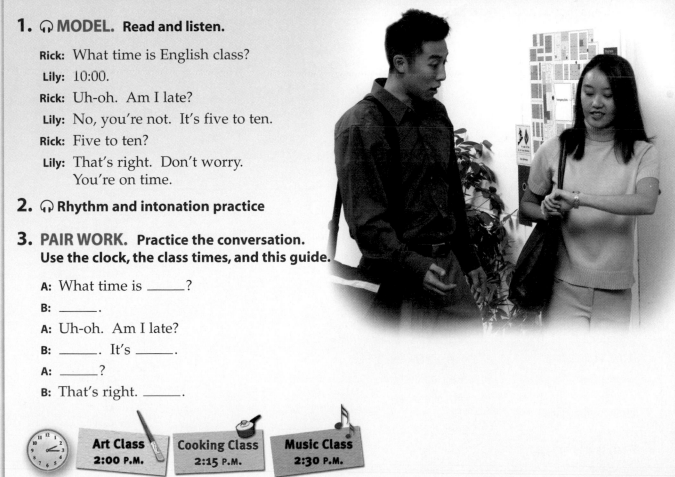

1. 🎧 **MODEL.** **Read and listen.**

Rick: What time is English class?
Lily: 10:00.
Rick: Uh-oh. Am I late?
Lily: No, you're not. It's five to ten.
Rick: Five to ten?
Lily: That's right. Don't worry.
You're on time.

2. 🎧 **Rhythm and intonation practice**

3. PAIR WORK. **Practice the conversation.**
Use the clock, the class times, and this guide.

A: What time is _____?
B: _____.
A: Uh-oh. Am I late?
B: _____. It's _____.
A: _____?
B: That's right. _____.

Art Class 2:00 P.M.

Cooking Class 2:15 P.M.

Music Class 2:30 P.M.

37

2 ▷ Invite Someone to an Event

A ◌ **VOCABULARY. Events.** Listen and practice.

1. a movie

2. a play

3. a concert

4. a party

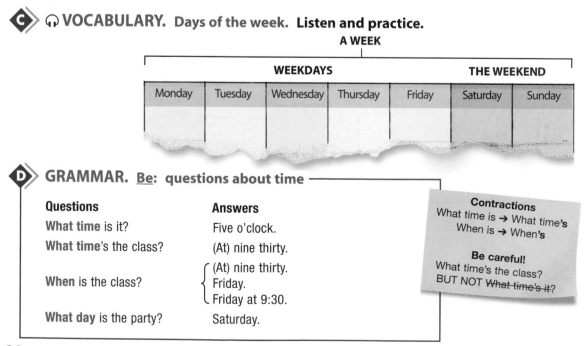
5. a game

6. a speech

📖 **VOCABULARY BOOSTER** See page V2 for more.

B ◌ **LISTENING COMPREHENSION.** Listen to the conversations about events. Check ☑ the time.

1. the concert
☐ 2:30 ☐ 8:30

2. the game
☐ 3:30 ☐ 3:15

3. the play
☐ 6:00 ☐ 7:00

4. the movie
☐ 9:15 ☐ 9:50

5. the party
☐ 12:00 A.M. ☐ 12:00 P.M.

6. the speech
☐ 12:00 A.M. ☐ 12:00 P.M.

C ◌ **VOCABULARY. Days of the week.** Listen and practice.

A WEEK

	WEEKDAYS				THE WEEKEND	
Monday	Tuesday	Wednesday	Thursday	Friday	Saturday	Sunday

D **GRAMMAR. Be:** questions about time

Questions

What time is it?

What time's the class?

When is the class?

What day is the party?

Answers

Five o'clock.

(At) nine thirty.

⎰ (At) nine thirty.
⎱ Friday.
⎱ Friday at 9:30.

Saturday.

Contractions
What time is → What time's
When is → When's

Be careful!
What time's the class?
BUT NOT ~~What time's it?~~

E ▸ Complete the questions.

1. A: When _____ the party?
   B: 11:00.

2. A: _____ day is the game?
   B: Saturday.

3. A: What _____ is the concert?
   B: 8:00.

4. A: What _____ is the speech?
   B: Tuesday.

5. A: _____ time is it?
   B: 2:30.

6. A: _____ is the play?
   B: Friday at 9:00.

F ▸ 🎧 LISTENING COMPREHENSION. Listen. Write the events on the calendar.

Monday		Thursday	
5:30		5:30	
6:30		6:30	
7:00		7:00	speech
7:15		7:15	

Tuesday		Friday	
5:30		5:30	
6:30		6:30	
7:00		7:00	
7:15		7:15	

Wednesday		Saturday		Sunday	
5:30		5:30		5:30	
6:30		6:30		6:30	
7:00		7:00		7:00	
7:15		7:15		7:15	

CONVERSATION • *Invite someone to an event.*

1. 🎧 MODEL. Read and listen.

Craig: There's a play on Tuesday—*The Apartment*. Would you like to go?
Debbie: Sounds great. What time?
Craig: 7:00.
Debbie: OK. Let's meet at a quarter to seven.

2. 🎧 Rhythm and intonation practice

3. PAIR WORK. Practice the conversation in your own way. Use the ads or real information.

A: There's a _____ on _____—_____. Would you like to go?
B: Sounds great. What time?
A: _____.
B: OK. Let's meet at _____.

BASKETBALL GAME
BRAZIL and CANADA
Saturday, 8:30 P.M.

Madhur Jaffrey SPEAKS
Wednesday, 8:00

WEEKEND CONCERT
THE TOKYO STRINGS
SUNDAY, 3:30 P.M.

ENGLISH MOVIE FESTIVAL
About a Boy
starring **Hugh Grant**
THURSDAY, 6:00

39

Talk about Dates

A 🎧 **VOCABULARY.** Months of the year. Listen and practice. What month is <u>your</u> birthday?

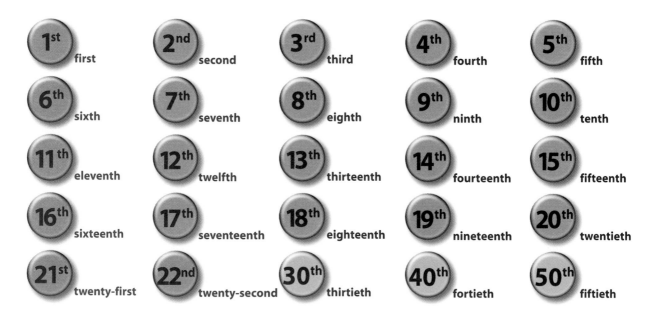

B 🎧 **VOCABULARY.** Ordinal numbers. Listen and practice.

1st first	**2nd** second	**3rd** third	**4th** fourth	**5th** fifth
6th sixth	**7th** seventh	**8th** eighth	**9th** ninth	**10th** tenth
11th eleventh	**12th** twelfth	**13th** thirteenth	**14th** fourteenth	**15th** fifteenth
16th sixteenth	**17th** seventeenth	**18th** eighteenth	**19th** nineteenth	**20th** twentieth
21st twenty-first	**22nd** twenty-second	**30th** thirtieth	**40th** fortieth	**50th** fiftieth

C 🎧 **LISTENING COMPREHENSION.** Listen to the dates. Circle the dates on the calendar in Exercise A.

D **PAIR WORK.** Take turns saying and writing dates from the calendar in Exercise A.

July thirty-first

July 31st

GRAMMAR. Prepositions of time and place

TIME

at	on	in
at 4:00	on March 12th	in January
at noon	on Monday	in the morning
at midnight	on the weekend	in the afternoon
at night	on a weekday	in the evening

PLACE

at	on	in *or* at
at 25 Bay St.	on Main Street	in / at the mall
at school	on the left	in / at Central Park
at work	on the corner	in / at the bus station

F **Complete the sentences. Use prepositions.**

1. The concert is _on_ July 14th _____ 3:00 _____ the afternoon.

2. The speech is _____ December 6th _____ 4:00 _____ the museum.

3. The basketball game is _____ Tuesday _____ the park _____ Smith St.

4. The party is _____ school _____ October 31st _____ midnight.

5. The movie is _____ 6:00 _____ the evening.

CONVERSATION • *Talk about dates.*

1. ⌒ **MODEL. Read and listen.**

   Carol: When's your birthday?

   Tom: On July 15th. When's yours?

   Carol: My birthday's in November. November 13th.

2. ⌒ **Rhythm and intonation practice**

3. **PAIR WORK. Practice the conversation. Use _your_ birthday.**

   A: When's your birthday?

   B: _____. When's yours?

   A: My birthday's _____.

   Now ask about other people's birthdays.

   Ideas

your brother / sister
your mother / father
your teacher

41

TOP NOTCH WEBSITE
For Unit 5 online activities, visit the
Top Notch Companion Website at
www.longman.com/topnotch.

A ◠ **READING. Read and listen. What events are there this week?**

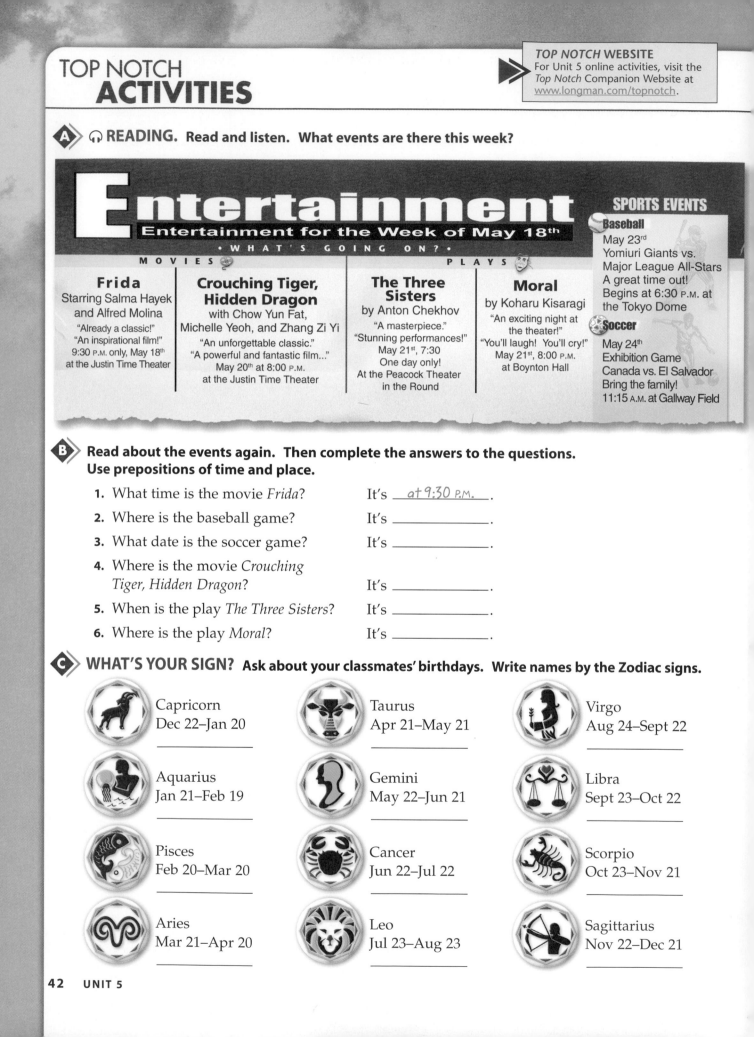

Entertainment
Entertainment for the Week of May 18th
• W H A T ' S   G O I N G   O N ? •

M O V I E S

Frida
Starring Salma Hayek
and Alfred Molina
"Already a classic!"
"An inspirational film!"
9:30 P.M. only, May 18th
at the Justin Time Theater

**Crouching Tiger,
Hidden Dragon**
with Chow Yun Fat,
Michelle Yeoh, and Zhang Zi Yi
"An unforgettable classic."
"A powerful and fantastic film..."
May 20th at 8:00 P.M.
at the Justin Time Theater

P L A Y S

**The Three
Sisters**
by Anton Chekhov
"A masterpiece."
"Stunning performances!"
May 21st, 7:30
One day only!
At the Peacock Theater
in the Round

Moral
by Koharu Kisaragi
"An exciting night at
the theater!"
"You'll laugh! You'll cry!"
May 21st, 8:00 P.M.
at Boynton Hall

SPORTS EVENTS

Baseball
May 23rd
Yomiuri Giants vs.
Major League All-Stars
A great time out!
Begins at 6:30 P.M. at
the Tokyo Dome

Soccer
May 24th
Exhibition Game
Canada vs. El Salvador
Bring the family!
11:15 A.M. at Gallway Field

B **Read about the events again. Then complete the answers to the questions.
Use prepositions of time and place.**

1. What time is the movie *Frida*?   It's ___at 9:30 P.M.___.

2. Where is the baseball game?   It's _____.

3. What date is the soccer game?   It's _____.

4. Where is the movie *Crouching
   Tiger, Hidden Dragon*?   It's _____.

5. When is the play *The Three Sisters*?   It's _____.

6. Where is the play *Moral*?   It's _____.

C **WHAT'S YOUR SIGN?** **Ask about your classmates' birthdays. Write names by the Zodiac signs.**

Capricorn
Dec 22–Jan 20
_____

Taurus
Apr 21–May 21
_____

Virgo
Aug 24–Sept 22
_____

Aquarius
Jan 21–Feb 19
_____

Gemini
May 22–Jun 21
_____

Libra
Sept 23–Oct 22
_____

Pisces
Feb 20–Mar 20
_____

Cancer
Jun 22–Jul 22
_____

Scorpio
Oct 23–Nov 21
_____

Aries
Mar 21–Apr 20
_____

Leo
Jul 23–Aug 23
_____

Sagittarius
Nov 22–Dec 21
_____

- **Vocabulary.** Look at the picture and name the events.
  A concert, a game . . .

- **Grammar.** Write statements with <u>There's a</u> . . .
  There's a concert on Tuesday at _____ . . .

- **Social language.** Create conversations for the people about the times and days of the events.
  A: What time is the concert?
  B: It's at . . .

Welcome
Amanda Roy, writer
When: 2:00
Friday, May 20
Where: Weekday Books

Chubu University vs. Ohio University
Sunday, May 22 at noon
Star Stadium
12 21st Street

JUICE in Concert
When: Tuesday, May 24
8:30 P.M.
Where: Gemini Stadium

Party
Welcome all students!
Saturday, May 28
9:30 P.M.
Where? 58 Post Street
(across from bank)

MAY
20
FRIDAY

✔	Now I can . . .
☐	talk about time.
☐	invite someone to an event.
☐	talk about dates.

43

Clothes

1 *Identify Clothes*

A 🎧 **VOCABULARY.** Clothes. Listen and practice.

1. a shoe 2. a shirt 3. a sweater

4. a tie 5. a jacket 6. a skirt 7. a dress 8. a blouse 10. a suit
9. pants*

* <u>Pants</u> is a plural noun.

📖 **VOCABULARY BOOSTER** See page V3 for more.

B 🎧 **PRONUNCIATION.** Plural nouns. Listen and practice.

1. /s/   **2.** /z/   **3.** /ɪz/
shirt**s** = shirt/s/   shoe**s** = shoe/z/   blouse**s** = blouse/ɪz/
jacket**s** = jacket/s/   sweater**s** = sweater/z/   dresse**s** = dress/ɪz/

C **GRAMMAR.** <u>This</u>, <u>that</u>, <u>these</u>, <u>those</u>

this tie   **that** tie   **these** shoes   **those** shoes

D Look at the pictures. Write <u>this</u>, <u>that</u>, <u>these</u>, or <u>those</u> and the name of the clothes.

1. *those jackets*

2. _____

3. _____

4. _____

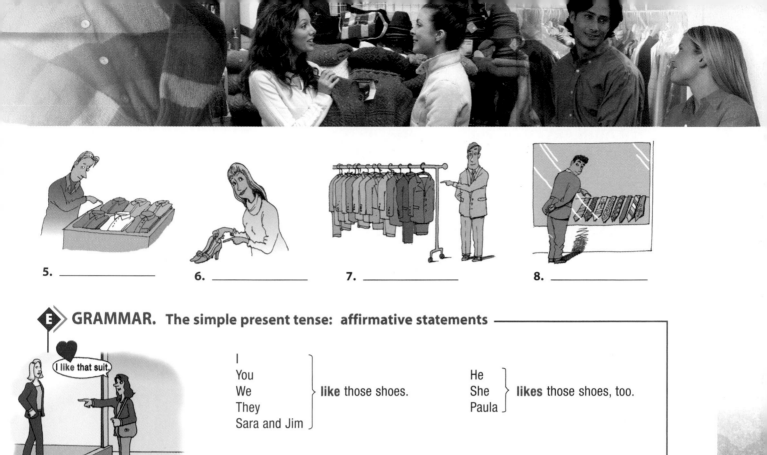

5. _____ **6.** _____ **7.** _____ **8.** _____

E▸ GRAMMAR. The simple present tense: affirmative statements

I
You
We
They
Sara and Jim
} **like** those shoes.

He
She
Paula
} **likes** those shoes, too.

I like that suit.

F▸ Complete each statement with <u>like</u> or <u>likes</u>.

1. We ___*like*___ this sweater.

2. She _____ those jackets.

3. They _____ that tie.

4. Helen _____ those dresses.

5. I _____ these sweaters.

6. He _____ that suit.

CONVERSATION • *Give and accept compliments about clothes.*

1. ⌒ **MODEL. Read and listen.**

Marie: I like that dress.

Jane: Thank you.

Marie: You're welcome.

2. ⌒ **Rhythm and intonation practice**

3. PAIR WORK. Compliment classmates on their clothes.

A: I like _____.

B: _____.

A: You're welcome.

45

Talk about Wants and Needs

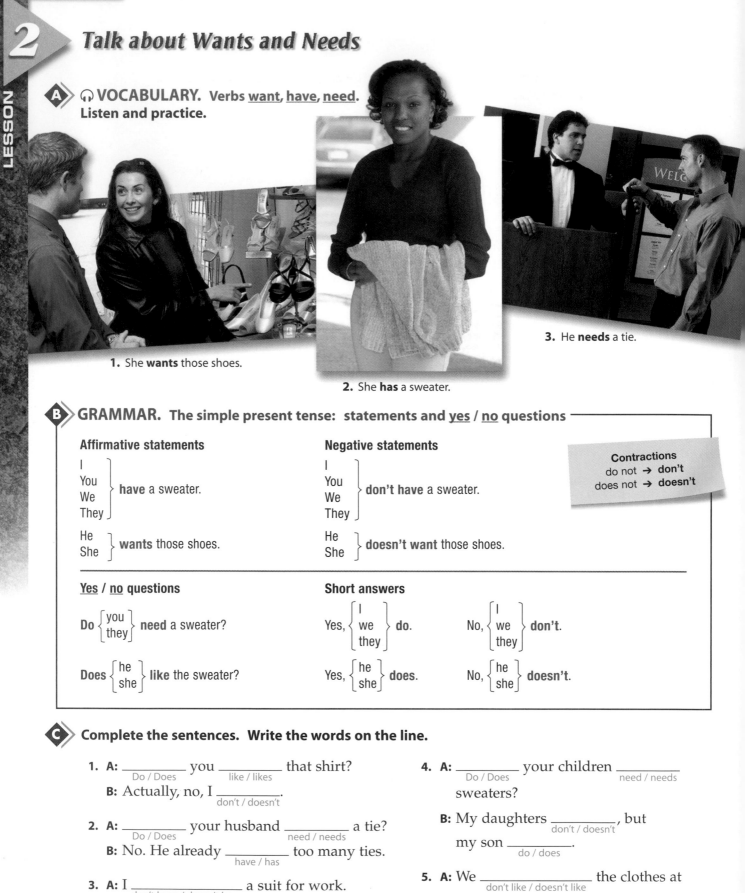

A 🎧 **VOCABULARY.** Verbs <u>want</u>, <u>have</u>, <u>need</u>. Listen and practice.

1. She **wants** those shoes.

2. She **has** a sweater.

3. He **needs** a tie.

B **GRAMMAR.** The simple present tense: statements and <u>yes</u> / <u>no</u> questions

Affirmative statements

I
You
We
They
} **have** a sweater.

He
She
} **wants** those shoes.

Negative statements

I
You
We
They
} **don't have** a sweater.

He
She
} **doesn't want** those shoes.

Contractions
do not → **don't**
does not → **doesn't**

Yes / **no** questions

Do { you / they } **need** a sweater?

Does { he / she } **like** the sweater?

Short answers

Yes, { I / we / they } **do**.

No, { I / we / they } **don't**.

Yes, { he / she } **does**.

No, { he / she } **doesn't**.

C Complete the sentences. Write the words on the line.

1. **A:** _____ you _____ that shirt?
   <u>Do / Does</u>   <u>like / likes</u>
   B: Actually, no, I _____.
   <u>don't / doesn't</u>

2. **A:** _____ your husband _____ a tie?
   <u>Do / Does</u>   <u>need / needs</u>
   B: No. He already _____ too many ties.
   <u>have / has</u>

3. **A:** I _____ a suit for work.
   <u>don't have / doesn't have</u>
   B: You _____ one!
   <u>need / needs</u>

4. **A:** _____ your children _____
   <u>Do / Does</u>   <u>need / needs</u>
   sweaters?
   B: My daughters _____, but
   <u>don't / doesn't</u>
   my son _____.
   <u>do / does</u>

5. **A:** We _____ the clothes at
   <u>don't like / doesn't like</u>
   this mall.
   B: Really? That's too bad.

⌒ **LISTENING COMPREHENSION.** Listen to the conversations about clothes. Check ☑ each statement <u>True</u> or <u>False</u>.

	True	False
1. They like the sweater.	☑	☐
2. He doesn't need shoes.	☐	☐
3. They don't want the suit.	☐	☐
4. He needs a jacket in the restaurant.	☐	☐
5. He needs a tie, too.	☐	☐

CONVERSATION • *Compare opinions about clothes.*

1. ⌒ **MODEL.** Read and listen.

Linda: Do you like this sweater?
Beth: Yes, I do.

Linda: And do you like those shoes?
Beth: No, I don't. Do you?
Linda: Actually, I think they're very nice.

2. ⌒ **Rhythm and intonation practice**

3. **PAIR WORK.** Now talk about the pictures.

A: Do you like _____?
B: _____.
A: And do you like _____?
B: _____.

4. **DISCUSSION.** Point to the pictures and tell the class about your partner.

> ❝Ellen likes these shoes.
> She doesn't like this suit. ❞

47

3 Describe Clothes

A 🎧 VOCABULARY. Colors and other descriptive adjectives. Listen and practice.

1. red
2. orange
3. yellow
4. green
5. blue
6. purple
7. white
8. black
9. gray
10. brown

11. a **new** dress

12. an **old** dress

13. **clean** shoes

14. **dirty** shoes

15. a **beautiful** tie

B GRAMMAR. Adjectives

Use adjectives with the verb <u>be</u>.

The shirt is **white**.   The shirts are **white**.

Use adjectives before nouns.

It's a **white** shirt.   NOT ~~It's a shirt white.~~

Be careful: Don't add <u>-s</u> to adjectives.

They're white shirts.   NOT ~~They're whites shirts.~~

C Write two descriptions for each picture. Use an adjective. Use <u>It's</u> or <u>They're</u>.

1. The __blouses__ are __white__.
   __They're white blouses__.

2. The _____ is _____.
   _____.

3. The _____ is _____.
   _____.

4. The _____ are _____.
   _____.

D On a separate piece of paper, write about five classmates.

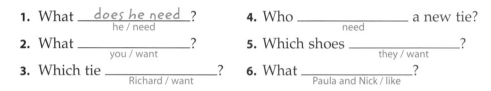

1. Allen has a gray shirt and black shoes. They're new shoes.

E **GRAMMAR.** The simple present tense: information questions

Who has a red shirt?	Jack does.
What does Ben need?	New shoes.
Which shoes do you like?	The black shoes.
When do they want the shoes?	On Tuesday.

F Complete each question, using the simple present tense.

1. What ___does he need___ ?
   _{he / need}

2. What _____?
   _{you / want}

3. Which tie _____?
   _{Richard / want}

4. Who _____ a new tie?
   _{need}

5. Which shoes _____?
   _{they / want}

6. What _____?
   _{Paula and Nick / like}

CONVERSATION • *Talk about shopping for clothes.*

1. ⌒ **MODEL.** **Read and listen.**

Tony: Let's go shopping.

Heidi: OK. What do you need?

Tony: I need a tie and a new suit.

Heidi: Is that all?

Tony: Yes, it is. Oh, actually I need shoes too!

2. ⌒ **Rhythm and intonation practice**

3. **PAIR WORK.** Role-play your <u>own</u> conversation. Use the pictures and the guide, or create a new conversation.

A: Let's go shopping.

B: OK. What do you _____?

A: I _____.

B: Is that all?

A: _____ . . .

Continue in your <u>own</u> way . . .

TOP NOTCH
ACTIVITIES

A 🎧 **READING.** Read and listen to the advertisement from today's newspaper. Which clothes do you like?

The Emporium *A Great Clothes Store!*

TODAY ONLY! ½ PRICE SALE

MEN'S AND WOMEN'S CLOTHES

All stores open until midnight. Low, low prices!

White not available at Central Station location.

Many more styles available!

Other sale items today: children's jackets and shoes.

Store locations:
27 Park Street
The City Mall
Central Station
No phone orders.

Other colors available: black and yellow.

Brown at Park Street store only.

B Complete each statement, based on the reading.

1. The Emporium is a great _____ store.
2. The sale is _____ only.
3. The Emporium also has black and yellow men's _____.
4. _____ sweaters are available at the Park Street store only.
5. There are women's blouses in three _____: white, red, and blue.
6. Children's _____ and _____ are also on sale today at the Emporium.

C **PAIR WORK.** Talk to your partner about the sale at the Emporium. Use the advertisement.

❝ What do you need? ❞

❝ I need sweaters, and my husband wants a new tie. Let's go shopping. ❞

NEED HELP? Here's language you already know:

Do you want _____?
Do you like _____?
Do you have _____?
What do you need?
Which _____ do you like?

TOP NOTCH WEBSITE
For Unit 6 online activities, visit the *Top Notch* Companion Website at www.longman.com/topnotch.

- **Vocabulary.** Describe the clothes and shoes.
  Those shoes are beautiful.

- **Grammar.** Ask your partner questions about the picture.
  Do you like this blue tie?

- **Social language.** Create conversations for the people.
  A: Let's go shopping.
  B: OK. What do you need?

LATER

Now I can...
- ☐ identify clothes.
- ☐ talk about wants and needs.
- ☐ describe clothes.

51

UNIT 7

Home and Work

UNIT GOALS

1 Talk about where you live, work, or study
2 Describe your home
3 Name furniture and appliances

LESSON **1**

Talk about Where You Live, Work, or Study

A 🎧 **VOCABULARY.** Workplaces and homes. Listen and practice.

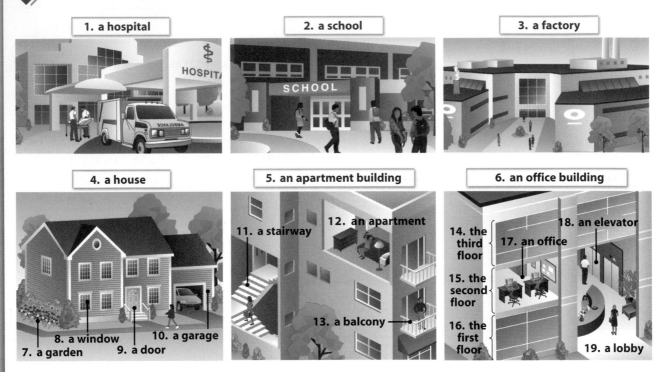

1. a hospital
2. a school
3. a factory
4. a house
5. an apartment building
6. an office building

11. a stairway
12. an apartment
13. a balcony

14. the third floor
15. the second floor
16. the first floor
17. an office
18. an elevator
19. a lobby

7. a garden
8. a window
9. a door
10. a garage

B **GRAMMAR.** Prepositions of place

in
She lives **in** an apartment.
I work **in** an office.

at
I live **at** 34 Circle Street.
He works **at** home.
She works **at** Smith Hospital.

on
He lives **on** Bank Street.
They live **on** the third floor.

across from

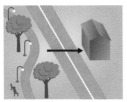

The house is **across from** the park.

around the corner from

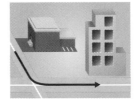

The office is **around the corner from** the school.

near

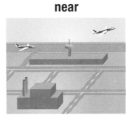

The factory is **near** the airport.

between

The restaurant is **between** Second Street and B Street.

C **Complete the sentences with prepositions of place. Use the map.**

1. Gail's apartment is ___on___ Taurus Street, ___near___ Central Park.

2. The hospital is _____ Gemini Street, _____ the school.

3. The school is _____ Fourth Avenue, _____ the park.

4. 3 Brothers Restaurant is _____ 82 Fifth Avenue, _____ Gemini Street and Taurus Street.

Gail's apartment
26

Taurus Street

3 Brothers Restaurant
82

School
85

Hospital
26

Fifth Avenue

Fourth Avenue

Central Park

Gemini Street

Nancy's house
20

Capricorn Street

CONVERSATION • *Talk about where you live, work, or study.*

1. 🎧 **MODEL. Read and listen.**

Sam: So what do you do?

Joe: I'm a student. I study at the Park School.

Sam: The Park School? Where's that?

Joe: On Second Street. Near the mall.

Sam: And do you live nearby?

Joe: Yes. I have an apartment near the school. What about you?

Sam: Me? I'm a chef. I work at Peter's Restaurant.

2. 🎧 **Rhythm and intonation practice**

3. **PAIR WORK. Exchange real information with your partner. Use the guide, or create a new conversation.**

A: So what do you do?

B: I'm _____. I _____.

A: _____? Where's that?

B: On _____. _____.

A: And _____? . . .

Continue in your <u>own</u> way . . .

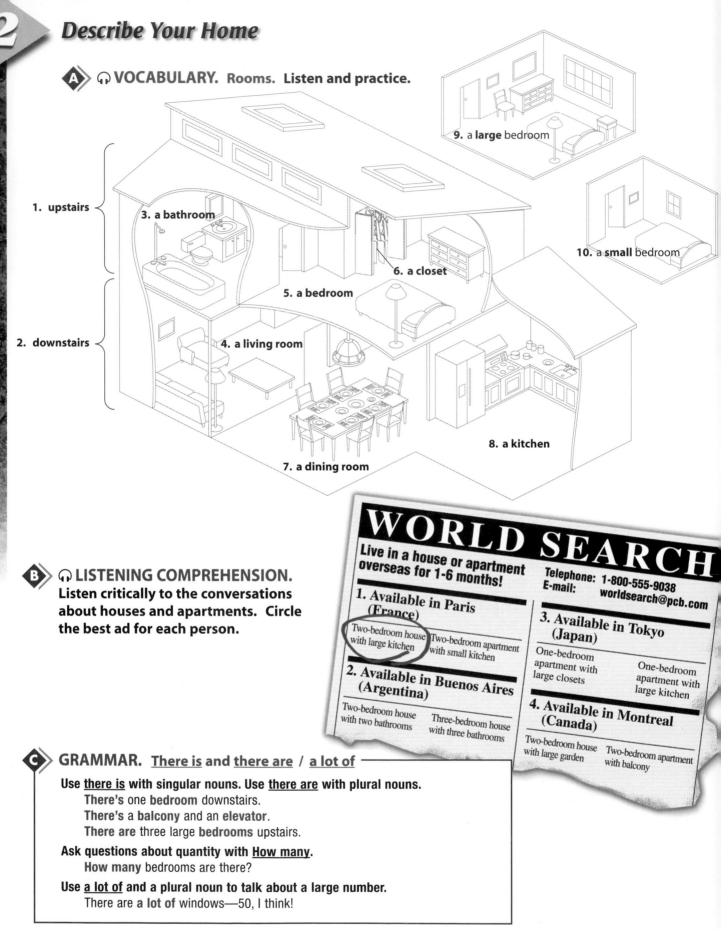

2 Describe Your Home

LESSON

A 🎧 **VOCABULARY.** Rooms. Listen and practice.

1. upstairs
2. downstairs
3. a bathroom
4. a living room
5. a bedroom
6. a closet
7. a dining room
8. a kitchen
9. a **large** bedroom
10. a **small** bedroom

B 🎧 **LISTENING COMPREHENSION.** Listen critically to the conversations about houses and apartments. Circle the best ad for each person.

WORLD SEARCH

Live in a house or apartment overseas for 1-6 months!

Telephone: 1-800-555-9038
E-mail: worldsearch@pcb.com

1. Available in Paris (France)

Two-bedroom house with large kitchen | Two-bedroom apartment with small kitchen

2. Available in Buenos Aires (Argentina)

Two-bedroom house with two bathrooms | Three-bedroom house with three bathrooms

3. Available in Tokyo (Japan)

One-bedroom apartment with large closets | One-bedroom apartment with large kitchen

4. Available in Montreal (Canada)

Two-bedroom house with large garden | Two-bedroom apartment with balcony

C **GRAMMAR.** <u>There is</u> and <u>there are</u> / <u>a lot of</u>

Use <u>there is</u> with singular nouns. Use <u>there are</u> with plural nouns.
There's one **bedroom** downstairs.
There's a **balcony** and an **elevator**.
There are three large **bedrooms** upstairs.

Ask questions about quantity with <u>How many</u>.
How many bedrooms are there?

Use <u>a lot of</u> and a plural noun to talk about a large number.
There are **a lot of** windows—50, I think!

D Complete the sentences. Use <u>there's</u>, <u>there are</u>, <u>is there</u>, or <u>are there</u>.

1. _Is there_ an elevator in your office?

2. _____ a lot of closets in my home.

3. _____ two bedrooms in their apartment.

4. This is a great house. _____ a garden?

5. _____ a garage and an elevator in her building.

6. _____ a balcony in your apartment?

E WRITING. Describe your dream house. On a separate piece of paper, write sentences with <u>there is</u> and <u>there are</u>. Use your own words.

> There are 25 bedrooms. There's a large garden. There are 10 bathrooms.

CONVERSATION · *Describe your home.*

1. 🎧 MODEL. Read and listen.

Rachel: Do you live in a house or an apartment?

Pat: An apartment.

Rachel: What's it like?

Pat: Well, there are three bedrooms and a large kitchen.

Rachel: Sounds nice!

2. 🎧 Rhythm and intonation practice

3. PAIR WORK. Exchange information about <u>your</u> home. Use the guide, or create a new conversation.

A: Do you live in a house or an apartment?

B: _____.

A: What's it like?

B: Well, there _____.

A: _____.

55

Name Furniture and Appliances

A 🎧 **VOCABULARY.** Furniture and appliances in the home and office. Listen and practice.

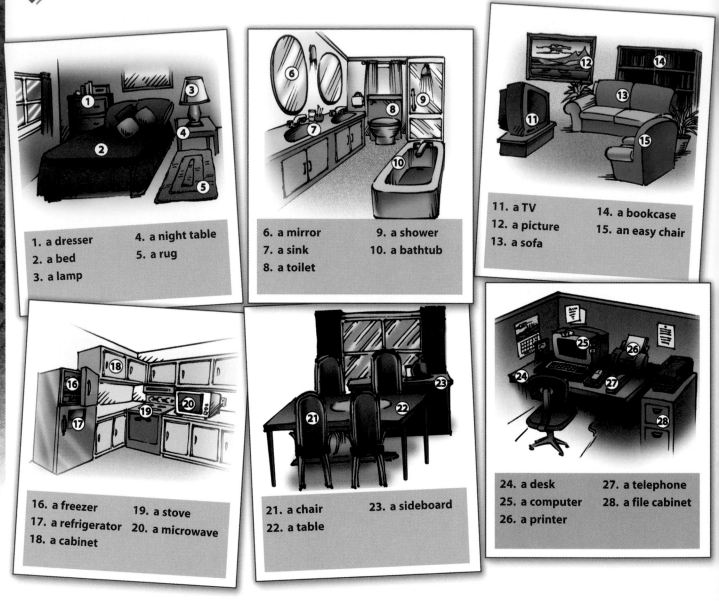

1. a dresser
2. a bed
3. a lamp
4. a night table
5. a rug

6. a mirror
7. a sink
8. a toilet
9. a shower
10. a bathtub

11. a TV
12. a picture
13. a sofa
14. a bookcase
15. an easy chair

16. a freezer
17. a refrigerator
18. a cabinet
19. a stove
20. a microwave

21. a chair
22. a table
23. a sideboard

24. a desk
25. a computer
26. a printer
27. a telephone
28. a file cabinet

📖 **VOCABULARY BOOSTER** See pages V4 and V5 for more.

B 🎧 **LISTENING COMPREHENSION.** Look back at Exercise A. Listen to the questions about furniture and appliances. Write which room they are in.

1. It's _in the kitchen_ .
2. It's _____ .
3. It's _____ .

4. It's _____ .
5. It's _____ .
6. It's _____ .

C **WHAT ABOUT YOU?** On a separate piece of paper, write the furniture and appliances you have in the rooms in <u>your</u> home.

🎧 **PRONUNCIATION.** <u>Th.</u> **There are two different sounds for <u>th</u> in English. Listen and practice.**

/θ/	/ð/
third	there
three	that
bath	mother

🎧 **Now listen and practice saying these sentences.**

1. There are three rooms on the third floor.
2. Their brother's house has three bathrooms.
3. This house has thirty-three bathtubs.

CONVERSATION • *Compare opinions about furniture.*

1. 🎧 **MODEL. Read and listen.**

Kim: Look at that easy chair. What do you think?

Irene: I think it's really nice.

Kim: You do?

Irene: Definitely. What about you?

Kim: I'm not sure.

2. 🎧 **Rhythm and intonation practice**

3. PAIR WORK. Ask for your partner's opinion about furniture. Use the pictures and the guide.

A: Look at that _____. What do you think?

B: I think it's _____.

A: You do?

B: Definitely. What about you?

A: _____.

🎧 Positive and negative adjectives

☺	☹
nice	awful
great	terrible
beautiful	ugly

TOP NOTCH
ACTIVITIES

TOP NOTCH WEBSITE
For Unit 7 online activities, visit the
Top Notch Companion Website at
www.longman.com/topnotch.

A 🎧 **READING.** Read and listen. Who lives in a house? Who lives in an apartment?

Ana Karina Espinel

My name is Ana Karina Espinel. I live in Cumbaya, Ecuador. My family has a very nice house with a two-car garage. It has a big, beautiful garden.

Downstairs there is a large living room, dining room, and a large kitchen. Upstairs there are four bedrooms. And we have a lot of bathrooms—five in all!

My mother also has an office upstairs. We love our house.

I'm Cem Korcan and I'm from Turkey. I live in a three-bedroom apartment in Istanbul. The building has a garage and a big garden.

I have one bathroom, a big living room, and a small kitchen. There's no dining room. It's a small apartment, but that's OK.

My favorite room is the living room. It has a beautiful view of Istanbul and the sea.

Cem Korcan

Soon-Ju Cho

I'm Soon-Ju Cho, from Korea. I'm a bank assistant. I live in a small house with my husband, Sun-Yoon Jong. We have three floors and a garage. There are two bedrooms, a small living room, a small kitchen, a dining room, and one bathroom.

My favorite room is the living room because it has a TV! I really want a garden, but unfortunately, we don't have one.

Source: Authentic *Top Notch* interviews

B Check ☑ the descriptions that match each person's home.

	three bedrooms	five bathrooms	a small kitchen	no dining room	no garden	a garage	an office
Ana Karina Espinel	☐	☐	☐	☐	☐	☐	☐
Cem Korcan	☐	☐	☐	☐	☐	☐	☐
Soon-Ju Cho	☐	☐	☐	☐	☐	☐	☐

C **DISCUSSION.** Which of the homes in the reading do you like?

> ❝ I like Ana's home. There's a big garden. ❞

D **WRITING.** On a separate piece of paper, compare <u>your</u> home with the homes in the reading.

> Mr. Korcan lives in an apartment. I live in an apartment, too.
>
> Ms. Espinel has five bathrooms, but I have one bathroom.

Info Gap. What things are different in the pictures? Ask your partner questions about his or her picture. Answer questions about your picture.

How many [lamps] are there in the bedroom? Is the sofa [green]?
Does the bathroom have a [shower]?

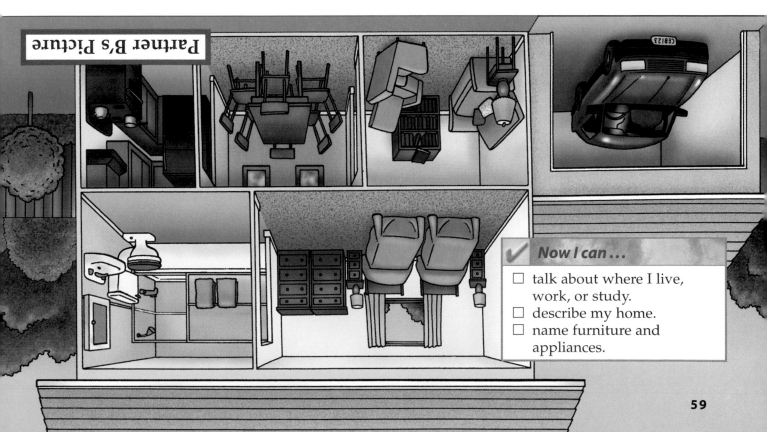

Partner A's Picture

Partner B's Picture

✓ **Now I can ...**

☐ talk about where I live, work, or study.
☐ describe my home.
☐ name furniture and appliances.

🎧 LISTENING COMPREHENSION. Listen to the conversations. Check ☑ each statement <u>True</u> or <u>False</u>. Then listen again to check your work.

	True	False
1. She's a manager.	☐	☐
2. He's a doctor.	☐	☐
3. She's an architect.	☐	☐
4. He's a student.	☐	☐
5. They're artists.	☐	☐
6. He's Mr. Clark.	☐	☐

 Write the name of each place.

1. <u>a restaurant</u>

4. _____

2. _____

5. _____

3. _____

6. _____

C PAIR WORK. Ask and answer questions about places on the map.
Then, on a separate piece of paper, write your questions and answers.

Where's the stadium?   It's across from the taxi stand.

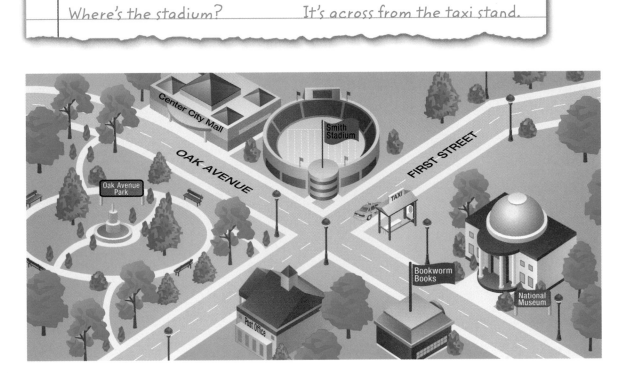

D Complete each sentence with a preposition of time or place.

1. The movie is ___on___ Friday ___at___ 7:50 ___in___ the evening.

2. The speech is _____ May 11th _____ the bookstore.

3. The travel agency is _____ the corner of State Street and First Avenue.

4. The play is _____ Saturday, _____ midnight.

5. The restaurant is _____ the left.

PAIR WORK • Introduce yourself to your partner.

Start like this: Hi. I'm ____.

💡 *Ideas*

Talk about:
• your occupations
• where you live

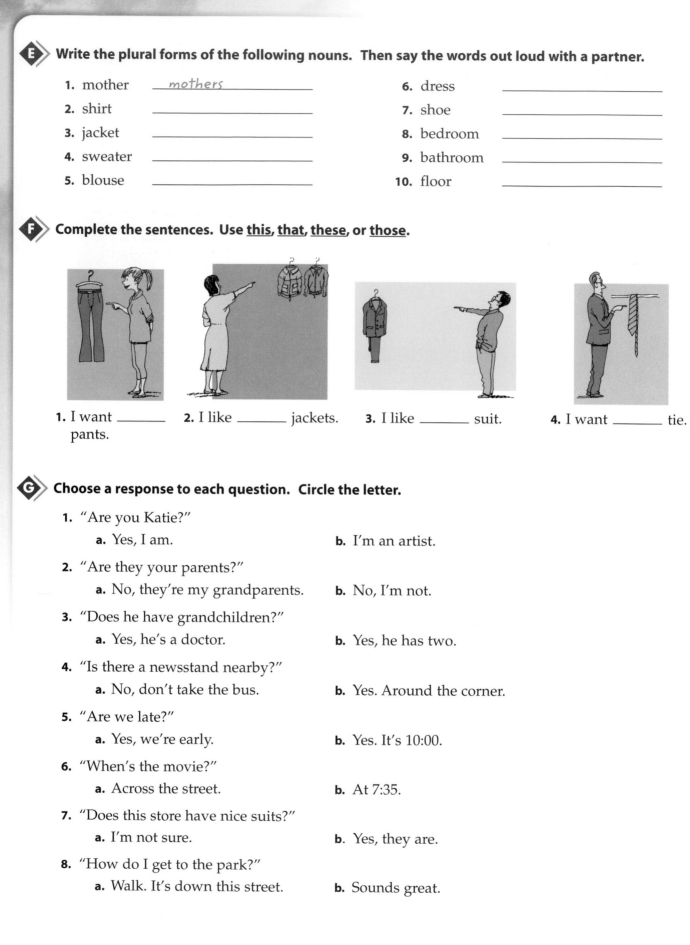

E ▸ **Write the plural forms of the following nouns. Then say the words out loud with a partner.**

1. mother   _mothers_ _____
2. shirt   _____
3. jacket   _____
4. sweater   _____
5. blouse   _____

6. dress   _____
7. shoe   _____
8. bedroom   _____
9. bathroom   _____
10. floor   _____

F ▸ **Complete the sentences. Use _this_, _that_, _these_, or _those_.**

1. I want _____ pants.   **2.** I like _____ jackets.   **3.** I like _____ suit.   **4.** I want _____ tie.

G ▸ **Choose a response to each question. Circle the letter.**

1. "Are you Katie?"
   a. Yes, I am.   **b.** I'm an artist.

2. "Are they your parents?"
   a. No, they're my grandparents.   **b.** No, I'm not.

3. "Does he have grandchildren?"
   a. Yes, he's a doctor.   **b.** Yes, he has two.

4. "Is there a newsstand nearby?"
   a. No, don't take the bus.   **b.** Yes. Around the corner.

5. "Are we late?"
   a. Yes, we're early.   **b.** Yes. It's 10:00.

6. "When's the movie?"
   a. Across the street.   **b.** At 7:35.

7. "Does this store have nice suits?"
   a. I'm not sure.   **b.** Yes, they are.

8. "How do I get to the park?"
   a. Walk. It's down this street.   **b.** Sounds great.

H ▸ **PAIR WORK.** Write your <u>own</u> response to each statement or question.
Then practice your exchanges with a partner.

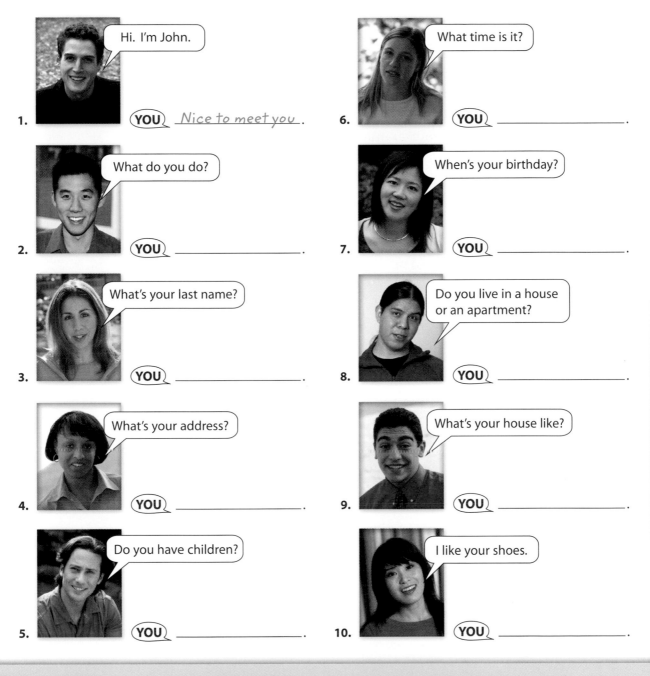

1. Hi. I'm John.
   YOU _Nice to meet you_.

2. What do you do?
   YOU _____.

3. What's your last name?
   YOU _____.

4. What's your address?
   YOU _____.

5. Do you have children?
   YOU _____.

6. What time is it?
   YOU _____.

7. When's your birthday?
   YOU _____.

8. Do you live in a house or an apartment?
   YOU _____.

9. What's your house like?
   YOU _____.

10. I like your shoes.
    YOU _____.

PAIR WORK • *Introduce your partner to other classmates.*

Start like this: ____, this is ____.

💡 *Ideas*

Ask about:
• occupations
• where you live
• family

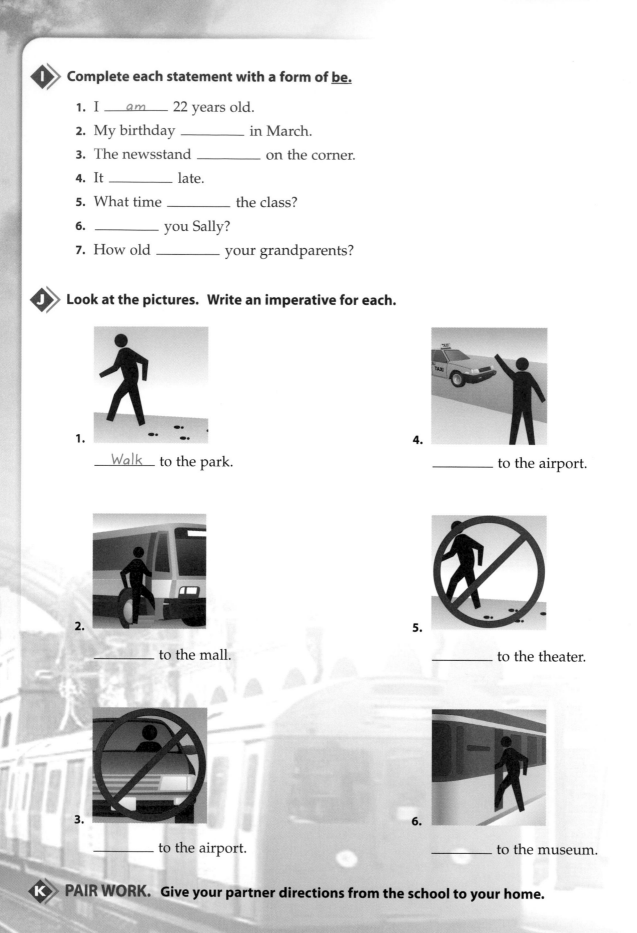

I ▷ **Complete each statement with a form of be.**

1. I ___am___ 22 years old.

2. My birthday _____ in March.

3. The newsstand _____ on the corner.

4. It _____ late.

5. What time _____ the class?

6. _____ you Sally?

7. How old _____ your grandparents?

J ▷ **Look at the pictures. Write an imperative for each.**

1.
   ___Walk___ to the park.

2.
   _____ to the mall.

3.
   _____ to the airport.

4.
   _____ to the airport.

5.
   _____ to the theater.

6.
   _____ to the museum.

K ▷ **PAIR WORK.** **Give your partner directions from the school to your home.**

L ▸ Check ☑ the <u>yes</u> / <u>no</u> questions.

☐ **1.** When is the movie?

☐ **2.** Is Martin a writer?

☐ **3.** Who is the teacher?

☐ **4.** Do you live in an apartment?

☐ **5.** Is there a newsstand nearby?

☐ **6.** Where's the movie?

☐ **7.** Do you like her shoes?

☐ **8.** Are you in this class?

M ▸ Write the sentences with contracted forms.

1. I am Ken. _____*I'm Ken*_____.

2. We are friends. _____.

3. When is the concert? _____?

4. Who is he? _____?

5. No, I am not. _____.

6. They do not like white shoes. _____.

7. You are welcome. _____.

N ▸ Underline the possessive adjectives in the following sentences.

1. Is Mr. Foley <u>your</u> lawyer?

2. Are we in your class?

3. Who are their parents?

4. He likes his sister's apartment.

5. My friends are your friends.

PAIR WORK • *Exchange real information about your families.*

Start like this: Tell me about your family.

Ideas

- Describe the people in your family.
- Talk about their occupations.
- Talk about where they live.

LISTENING COMPREHENSION. **Listen to the conversations and answer the questions. Listen again to check your work.**

1. What's his phone number?	
2. What's his last name?	
3. What time is it?	
4. Where's the post office?	
5. How old is his son?	

P **Complete each statement or question.**

1. Is he _____ husband?
   Beth / Beth's

2. Is this _____ apartment?
   their / they

3. Mr. Black is in _____ sister's house.
   her / his

4. _____ birthdays are in June.
   Our / We

5. How do you spell _____ name?
   you / your

Q **Write a question for each response.**

1. **A:** _Is she a teacher_ ?
   B: No. She's a student.

2. **A:** _____ ?
   B: I'm an architect.

3. **A:** _____ ?
   B: Yes. There's a restaurant across the street.

4. **A:** _____ ?
   B: It's 9:15.

5. **A:** _____ ?
   B: It's 34 Bank Street.

6. **A:** _____ ?
   B: The travel agency is at the corner of Martine and Fourth Street.

7. **A:** _____ ?
   B: It's in February. I'm a Pisces.

8. **A:** _____ ?
   B: They are my sisters.

R Write a short answer for each question.

1. Do you have a big family?_____.
2. Is there a post office nearby?_____.
3. Is Ms. Reilly your English teacher?_____.
4. Do you like red shoes?_____.
5. Do your children need new clothes?_____.

S Underline the subject pronouns in the following sentences.

1. He's a student.
2. Are you Amy?
3. Who is she?
4. Are they your parents?
5. It's around the corner.

T Complete each sentence with the correct verb.

1. We _____ friends.
   be / are
2. They _____ two children.
   has / have
3. Who _____ these blue suits?
   like / likes
4. _____ they _____ a big apartment?
   Do / Does   want / wants
5. When _____ Jack _____ those shirts?
   do / does   need / needs
6. _____ we on time?
   Is / Are

PAIR WORK • *Invite your partner to an event.*

Use real events in your town.
Start like this: There's a _____.
Would you like to go?

💡 *Ideas*

Talk about:
• a play
• a concert
• a movie
• your own idea:

UNIT GOALS

1 Describe your daily activities
2 Describe your schedule
3 Talk about how often you do things

Describe Your Daily Activities

A 🎧 **VOCABULARY.** Daily activities at home. **Listen and practice.**

1. get up

2. get dressed

3. brush my teeth

4. comb / brush my hair

5. shave

6. put on my makeup

7. eat breakfast

8. come home

9. make dinner

10. get undressed

11. take a shower / a bath

12. watch TV

13. go to bed

🎧 **MEALS**
breakfast
lunch
dinner

B **GRAMMAR.** The simple present tense: spelling rules with <u>he</u>, <u>she</u>, <u>it</u>

Add <u>-s</u> to most verbs with <u>he</u>, <u>she</u>, and <u>it</u>.

gets   makes   shaves   combs   plays

Add <u>-es</u> to verbs that end in -<u>s</u>, -<u>sh</u>, -<u>ch</u>, or -<u>x</u>.

bru<u>sh</u>es   wat<u>ch</u>es

But remember: do → **does**   go → **goes**   have → **has**   study → **studies**

C 🎧 **PRONUNCIATION.** Third-person singular verbs in the simple present tense. **Listen and practice the final sound of each word.**

1. /s/	**2.** /z/	**3.** /ɪz/
gets = get/s/	**shaves** = shave/z/	**watches** = watch/ɪz/
takes = take/s/	**comes** = come/z/	**brushes** = brush/ɪz/
eats = eat/s/	**needs** = need/z/	**practices** = practice/ɪz/

 Before and **after**

before 8:00   at 8:00   after 8:00

D Complete the sentences with daily activity verbs in the simple present tense. Then read the sentences aloud.

1. I get up at 6:00 A.M., but my wife _____ up at 7:00 A.M.

2. My wife _____ breakfast at 7:30.

3. When my wife is late for work, she _____ on her makeup on the train.

4. I don't watch TV, but my wife _____ TV after dinner.

5. I go to bed before 11:00 P.M., but my husband _____ to bed after 11:00.

6. I take a bath every morning, but my husband _____ a shower.

7. I make the bed on weekdays, and my husband _____ the bed on the weekend.

8. I brush my teeth twice a day, but my husband _____ his teeth three times a day.

E **WHAT ABOUT YOU?** On a separate piece of paper, write sentences about what you and the people in your family do every day.

CONVERSATION • *Describe your daily activities.*

1. **MODEL. Read and listen.**

   Yuka: Are you a morning person or an evening person?

   Melody: Me? I'm definitely an evening person.

   Yuka: Why do you say that?

   Melody: Well, I get up after ten. And I go to bed after two. What about you?

   Yuka: I'm a morning person. I get up at six.

2. **Rhythm and intonation practice**

3. **PAIR WORK. Compare your daily activities with a partner. Use the guide, or create a new conversation.**

   A: Are you a morning person or an evening person?

   B: Me? I'm _____.

   A: _____ . . .

   Continue the conversation about other daily activities.

2 Describe Your Schedule

A 🎧 **VOCABULARY.** Household chores and leisure activities. Listen and practice.

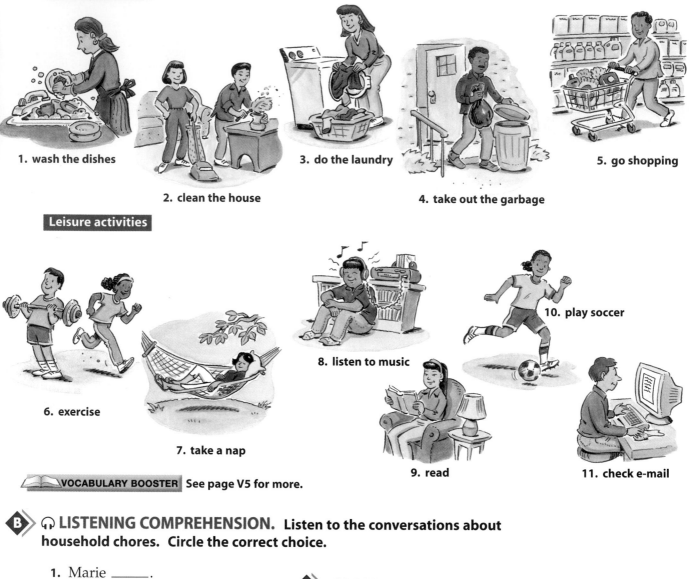

Household chores

1. wash the dishes
2. clean the house
3. do the laundry
4. take out the garbage
5. go shopping

Leisure activities

6. exercise
7. take a nap
8. listen to music
9. read
10. play soccer
11. check e-mail

📖 **VOCABULARY BOOSTER** See page V5 for more.

B 🎧 **LISTENING COMPREHENSION.** Listen to the conversations about household chores. Circle the correct choice.

1. Marie _____.
   a. cleans the apartment
   b. washes the dishes

2. Paul _____.
   a. takes out the garbage
   b. washes the dishes

3. Sue's brother _____.
   a. takes out the garbage
   b. does the laundry

4. Jen's husband _____.
   a. washes the dishes
   b. takes out the garbage

C **GRAMMAR.** The simple present tense: habitual activities

Use the simple present tense for habitual activities.

She checks her e-mail **every day**.

M	T	W	T	F	S	S
✓	✓	✓	✓	✓	✓	✓

He goes shopping **on Saturdays**.

M	T	W	T	F	S	S
					✓	
					✓	

Other time expressions

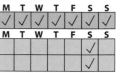

	M	T	W	T	F	S	S
once a week			✓				
twice a week			✓	✓			
three times a week			✓	✓		✓	

D. PAIR WORK. Ask your partner the questions. Add your own questions. Then write about your partner.

- When do you do the laundry?
- What do you do on the weekend?
- When does your family go shopping for food?
- When do you watch TV?

Alex does the laundry on Sundays.

CONVERSATION • *Describe your schedule.*

1. ⌕ MODEL. Read and listen.

Andy: What's your typical week like?

Sasha: Well, on Mondays and Wednesdays I go to school.

Andy: And what about the other days?

Sasha: On Tuesdays and Thursdays I work.

Andy: Sounds like you're pretty busy.

Sasha: Yes, I am. What about you?

Andy: I work every weekday. On the weekend I exercise and go to the movies.

2. ⌕ Rhythm and intonation practice

3. PAIR WORK. Write <u>your</u> typical weekly activities on the schedule. Then discuss your weekly schedules. Start like this:

A: What's your typical week like?

B: Well, _____.

A: And what about _____?

B: _____ . . .

Continue in your <u>own</u> way . . .

Monday

Tuesday

Wednesday

Thursday

Friday

Saturday

Sunday

3 ▶ Talk about How Often You Do Things

A ▶ **GRAMMAR.** Questions with <u>How often</u> / frequency adverbs ─────

Use <u>How often</u> to ask about frequency.

How often do you go out for dinner?	About three times a week.
How often does she visit her parents?	Every weekend.

Use frequency adverbs with the simple present tense.

100% ⬆ always

usually

sometimes

0% ⬇ never

I **always take** the bus to work.

Do you **usually take** the train to work?

He **sometimes exercises** in the morning.

My brother and his wife **never go** to concerts.

B ▶ ⌒ **LISTENING COMPREHENSION.** Listen to the interviews about how people get to work and school. Complete the chart. Then listen again to check your work.

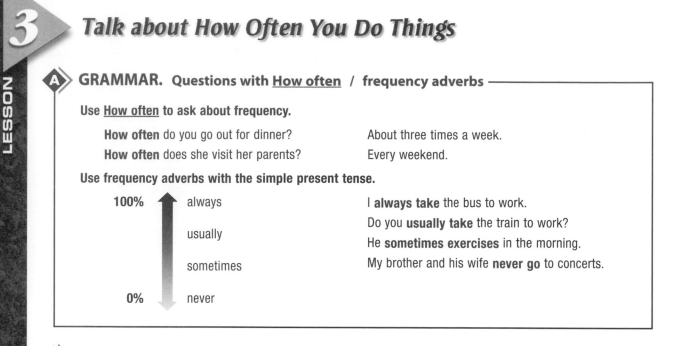

	Lynn	Matt	Jess	Frank
walks	☐	☐	☐	☐
drives	☐	☐	☐	☐
takes the bus	☐	☐	☐	☐
takes the train	☐	☐	☐	☐
takes a taxi	☐	☐	☐	☐

C ▶ **WHAT ABOUT YOU?** Write answers with frequency adverbs.

> *I usually walk to work.*

1. How do you go to school or work? _____.
2. When do you eat lunch and dinner? _____.
3. Do you take a nap in the afternoon? _____.

D **PAIR WORK.** Ask your partner questions. Complete the chart. Then tell the class about your partner.

How often do you:	You	Your partner
do the laundry?		
make dinner?		
go out for dinner?		
go to the movies?		
go dancing?		
practice speaking English?		

CONVERSATION • *Talk about how often you do things.*

1. ⌒ **MODEL.** Read and listen.

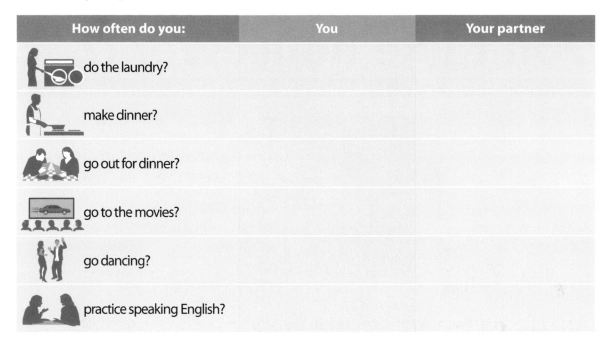

Bruce: Hi, Kevin. Long time no see.
Kevin: Hi, Bruce.
Bruce: Do you always take the bus?
Kevin: No, I usually walk.
Bruce: No wonder I never see you!

2. ⌒ **Rhythm and intonation practice**

3. **PAIR WORK.** Role-play running into a friend. Use the pictures and the guide, or create a new conversation.

A: Hi, _____. Long time no see.
B: Hi, _____.
A: Do you always _____?
B: No, I usually _____.
A: No wonder I never see you!

A 🎧 **READING.** Read and listen. Do you like housework?

Don't like housework?

CHECK OUT THESE NEW ROBOTS . . .

This is the iRobot Roomba Intelligent FloorVac®, or Roomba®. The Roomba is the world's first robot vacuum cleaner. How often do you clean your house? Once a week? The Roomba vacuums your rooms for you. You turn it on and it vacuums while you watch TV, exercise, or listen to music. Or while you sleep! The Roomba

Roomba

goes straight and it turns left or right. It turns if there is a sofa or a chair.

"Excellent! This is such a great idea!"
Judy Ruvo, New Zealand

This is the Auto Mower®. It's a robot that mows the lawn. You tell the robot what time you want it to work. How about after midnight, after you go to bed? It mows the lawn while you sleep. Or how about at noon? It mows the lawn while you have lunch. The Auto Mower can mow the lawn for 24 hours! Like the Roomba, it turns left and right, goes straight, and turns at the corner.

"What a robot!"
Mark Minor, U.K.

Auto Mower

Aibo

Meet Aibo®, the robot dog from SONY. Aibo doesn't vacuum. It doesn't mow the lawn. It doesn't do household chores like the laundry or the dishes. It dances and plays with a ball, and—like the Roomba and the Auto Mower—it moves around in the house or outside. Say, "Turn left," and it turns left.

"Great fun!" Chris Maverick, U.S.A.

Sources: http://www.onrobo.com, http://international.husqvarna.com, and http://www.us.aibo.com

B **WRITING.** Write sentences about the robots. Use the simple present tense of verbs from the box.

1. _The Roomba cleans the house_ .
2. _____ .
3. _____ .
4. _____ .
5. _____ .
6. _____ .

clean the house
mow the lawn
play with a ball
turn right and left
dance
do the laundry
wash the dishes

C **DISCUSSION.** Do you like the robots in the article? Which ones do you want? Why?

❝ I want the Roomba. I don't like housework. ❞

🎧 *TOP NOTCH* SONG
"Excuse Me, Please"
Lyrics on last book page.

TOP NOTCH WEBSITE
For Unit 8 online activities, visit the *Top Notch* Companion Website at www.longman.com/topnotch.

UNIT WRAP-UP

- **Vocabulary.** Study the pictures. Close your book. Tell your partner all the activities you remember.
  Get up, eat breakfast...

- **Tell a story.** Write about Jack Benson's daily activities. Use time expressions.
  Jack Benson gets up at 7:00 on weekdays.

Jack Benson
Typical Weekday

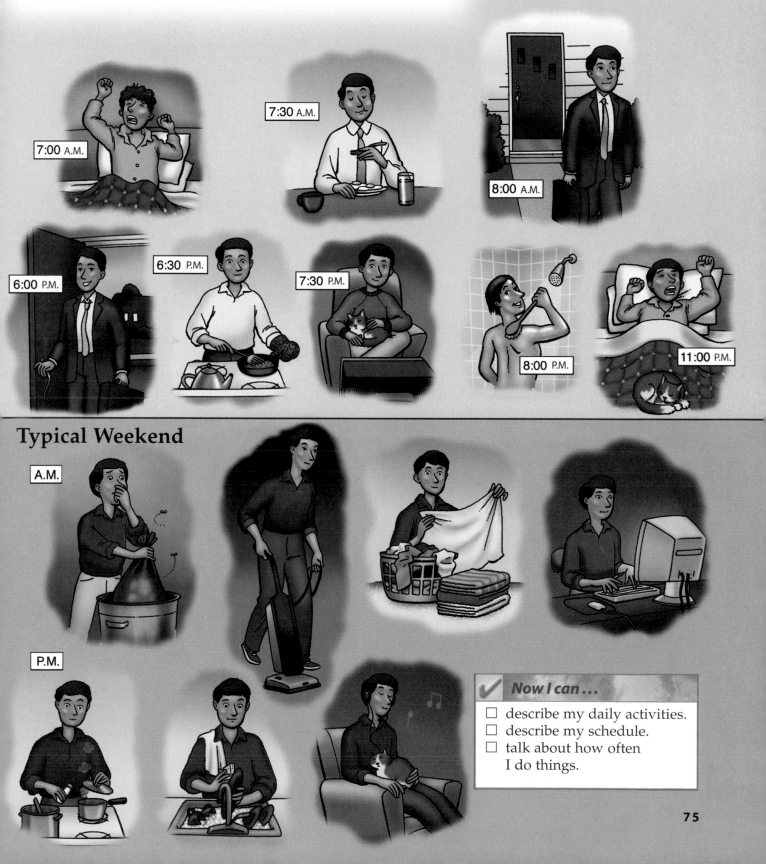

7:00 A.M.

7:30 A.M.

8:00 A.M.

6:00 P.M.

6:30 P.M.

7:30 P.M.

8:00 P.M.

11:00 P.M.

Typical Weekend

A.M.

P.M.

✔ Now I can ...

- ☐ describe my daily activities.
- ☐ describe my schedule.
- ☐ talk about how often I do things.

UNIT 9

Weather and Ongoing Activities

UNIT GOALS

1 Describe today's weather
2 Ask about people's activities
3 Discuss plans

LESSON 1

Describe Today's Weather

A 🎧 **VOCABULARY.** What's the weather like? Listen and practice.

1. It's cloudy.
2. It's sunny.
6. It's hot.
7. It's cold.

3. It's windy.

4. It's raining.
5. It's snowing.
8. It's warm.
9. It's cool.

📖 **VOCABULARY BOOSTER** See page V6 for more.

B 🎧 **LISTENING COMPREHENSION.** Listen. Check ☑️ today's weather in each of the cities. Then listen again. Write today's temperature.

	Hot	Warm	Cool	Cold	Temperature
Tokyo	✔				37°
London					
Mexico City					
Santiago					

Tokyo, Japan

C **PAIR WORK.** Describe the weather in <u>your</u> city today.

D **GRAMMAR.** The present continuous: affirmative and negative statements

The present continuous expresses actions in progress now. Use a form of <u>be</u> and a present participle.

Affirmative statements
It**'s raining**.
She**'s exercising** today.
They**'re wearing** sweaters.

Negative statements
It**'s not snowing**.
She**'s not studying**.
They**'re not wearing** jackets.

Present participles
wear → **wearing**
study → **studying**
exercise → **exercising**

 GRAMMAR. The present continuous: <u>yes</u> / <u>no</u> questions

Are you **reading** right now?	Yes, I am.	No, I'm not.
Is he **washing** the dishes?	Yes, he is.	No, he's not. [No, he isn't.]
Is it **raining**?	Yes, it is.	No, it's not. [No, it isn't.]
Are they **eating**?	Yes, they are.	No, they're not. [No, they aren't.]

F Complete the conversations with the present continuous.

1. **A:** *Are they cleaning* the house?
   _{they / clean}

   B: No, they ____. They _____ to music.
   _{listen}

2. **A:** _____ right now?
   _{you / work}

   B: No, we ____. We _____ TV.
   _{watch}

3. **A:** _____ English?
   _{she / study}

   B: No, she ____. She _____ her e-mail.
   _{check}

4. **A:** _____ the laundry?
   _{Mr. and Mrs. Reed / do}

   B: No, they ____. They _____ the dishes.
   _{wash}

CONVERSATION • *Describe today's weather.*

1. **MODEL.** Read and listen.

Paul: Hi, Manny. I'm calling from San Francisco. How's the weather in Lima?

Manny: Today? Awful. It's 18 degrees and raining.

Paul: No kidding. It's hot and sunny here!

2. **Rhythm and intonation practice**

3. **PAIR WORK.** Choose two cities. Then role-play a conversation. Use the guide, or create a new conversation.

A: Hi, ____. I'm calling from ____. How's the weather in ____?

B: Today? ____.

A: No kidding. It's ____ here!

💡 *Ideas*

Find the weather report in the newspaper. Or log onto www.weather.com.

International Express Airlines
Departures
Flight
003   Lima   7:30 A.M On Time

Information Center

Ask about People's Activities

A **GRAMMAR.** The present continuous: information questions

Who's driving?	Sarah is.
What are you **doing?**	Watching TV.
Where are Tim and Jack **going?**	They're going out for dinner.

B **PAIR WORK.** Ask your partner questions about Mike and Patty. Use the present continuous.

❝ It's 8:00. What's Patty doing? ❞

❝ She's taking a shower. ❞

C 🎧 **PRONUNCIATION.** Rising and falling intonation of questions. Use rising intonation for **yes / no** questions. Use falling intonation for information questions. Listen and practice.

<u>Yes / no</u> questions	Information questions
1. Are you reading?	What are you reading?
2. Is she driving?	Where is she driving?
3. Are they watching TV?	Who's watching TV?
4. Is your family here?	Where's your family?
5. Is there a pharmacy near here?	Where is there a pharmacy?

D **CHARADES.** One team mimes an activity. The other team asks questions. Use the activities from the box.

get up	get dressed	brush your teeth
comb your hair	take a shower	wash the dishes
drive	read	check e-mail
exercise	watch TV	listen to music
talk on the phone	go to bed	eat breakfast

Are you combing your hair?

GRAMMAR. The present participle: spelling rules

talk → **talking**   mak~~e~~ → **making**
read → **reading**   tak~~e~~ → **taking**
watch → **watching**   com~~e~~ → **coming**

But remember: shop → sho**pp**ing   get → ge**tt**ing

F **Write the present participles.**

1. read _____   3. wash _____   5. drive _____

2. write _____   4. go _____   6. get up _____

G 🎧 **LISTENING COMPREHENSION.** Listen. **Complete each statement in the present continuous.**

1. She's _watching TV_ with her father.   4. He's _____ for the kids.

2. He's _____ .   5. They're _____ to the museum.

3. She's _____ her mother.

CONVERSATION • *Make a polite phone call.*

1. 🎧 **MODEL.** **Read and listen.**

Jan: Hello?
Laura: Hi, Jan. This is Laura. What are you doing?
Jan: I'm feeding the kids.
Laura: Should I call you back later?
Jan: Yes, thanks. Talk to you later. Bye.
Laura: Bye.

2. 🎧 **Rhythm and intonation practice**

3. **PAIR WORK.** **Now role-play a call. Use the pictures and the guide, or create a new conversation.**

A: Hello?
B: Hi, _____. This is _____. What are you doing?
A: I'm _____.
B: Should I call you back later?
A: Yes, thanks. Talk to you later. Bye.
B: _____ .

Discuss Plans

THURSDAY
1. this morning
2. this afternoon
3. this evening
4. tonight

A 🎧 **VOCABULARY.** Time expressions. Listen and practice.

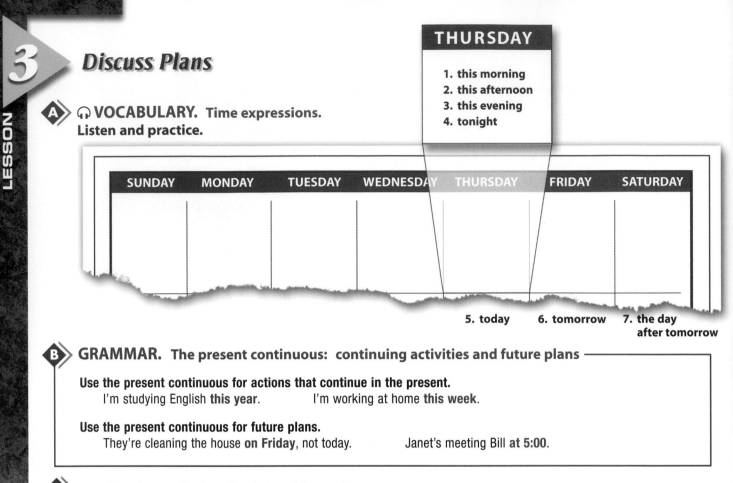

SUNDAY	MONDAY	TUESDAY	WEDNESDAY	THURSDAY	FRIDAY	SATURDAY

5. today   6. tomorrow   7. the day after tomorrow

B **GRAMMAR.** The present continuous: continuing activities and future plans

Use the present continuous for actions that continue in the present.
I'm studying English **this year**.   I'm working at home **this week**.

Use the present continuous for future plans.
They're cleaning the house **on Friday**, not today.   Janet's meeting Bill **at 5:00**.

C Read Beth Rand's date book for this week.

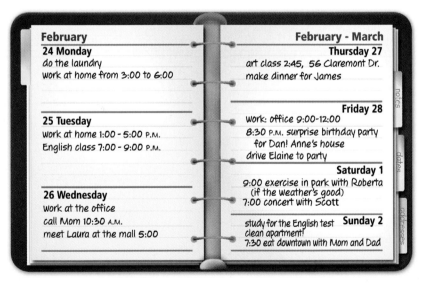

February

24 Monday
do the laundry
work at home from 3:00 to 6:00

25 Tuesday
work at home 1:00 – 5:00 P.M.
English class 7:00 – 9:00 P.M.

26 Wednesday
work at the office
call Mom 10:30 A.M.
meet Laura at the mall 5:00

February - March

Thursday 27
art class 2:45, 56 Claremont Dr.
make dinner for James

Friday 28
work: office 9:00-12:00
8:30 P.M. surprise birthday party
for Dan! Anne's house
drive Elaine to party

Saturday 1
9:00 exercise in park with Roberta
(if the weather's good)
7:00 concert with Scott

Sunday 2
study for the English test
clean apartment!
7:30 eat downtown with Mom and Dad

Now complete each statement with the present continuous. Use the affirmative and negative.

1. On Monday, Beth ___is doing the laundry___ and ___working at home___
   from 3:00 to 6:00.

2. On Tuesday, she _____ from 1:00 to 5:00.

3. The next day, Wednesday, she _____ Laura at the mall.

4. Thursday afternoon, she _____ at 2:45.

5. Later that day, she _____ for James.

6. On Friday, at 8:30, Beth _____ to Dan's party.

7. Beth _____ Elaine to the party.

8. On Saturday morning, Beth _____ in the park with Roberta.

9. In the evening, she _____ with Scott.

10. On Sunday, she _____ and _____.

11. On Sunday night, she _____ downtown with her parents.

CONVERSATION • *Discuss plans.*

1. ⌖ **MODEL. Read and listen.**

Scott: So what are you doing this weekend?

Dan: I'm not sure. What about you?

Scott: Well, on Saturday, if the weather is good, I'm meeting Pam in the park.

Dan: Do you want to get together on Sunday? I'm not doing anything special.

Scott: Sure. Call me Sunday morning.

2. ⌖ **Rhythm and intonation practice**

3. **WHAT ABOUT YOU?** Fill in the date book for this week. Write your activities and the times.

_____
Monday

_____
Tuesday

_____
Wednesday

_____
Thursday

_____
Friday

_____
Saturday

_____
Sunday

4. **PAIR WORK.** Now make plans with your partner. Use your date book. Use this guide, or create a new conversation.

A: So what are you doing _____?

B: _____. What about you?

A: Well, _____.

B: Do you want to get together _____? I'm not doing anything special.

A: _____. Call me _____.

TOP NOTCH
ACTIVITIES

A 🎧 **READING.** Read and listen to the instant messages.

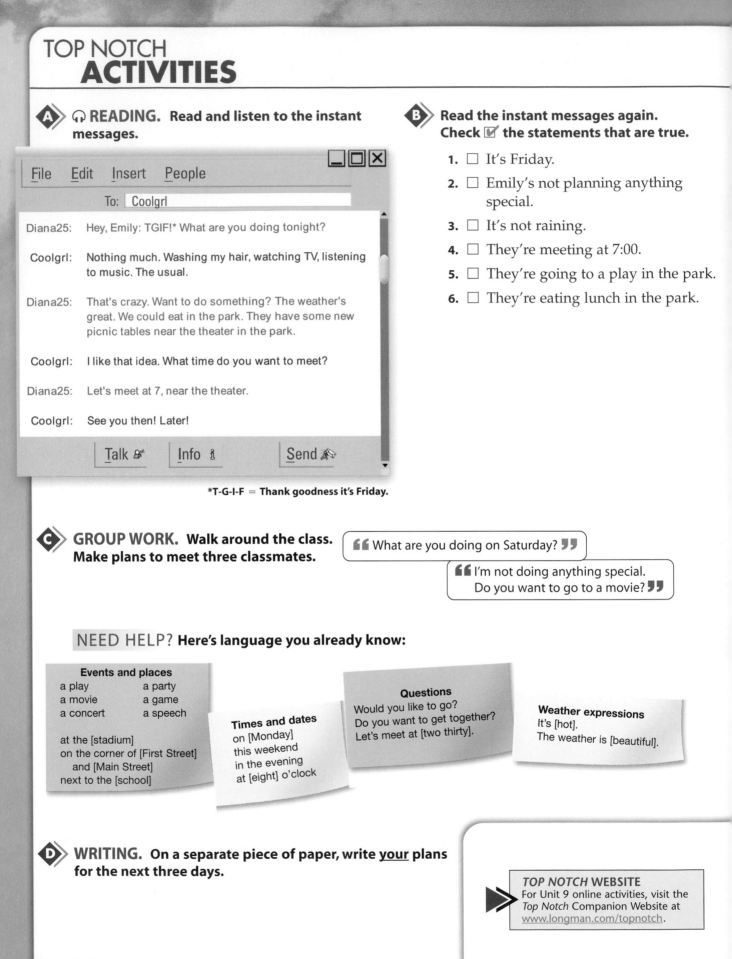

File   Edit   Insert   People

To: Coolgrl

Diana25:   Hey, Emily: TGIF!* What are you doing tonight?

Coolgrl: Nothing much. Washing my hair, watching TV, listening to music. The usual.

Diana25:   That's crazy. Want to do something? The weather's great. We could eat in the park. They have some new picnic tables near the theater in the park.

Coolgrl: I like that idea. What time do you want to meet?

Diana25:   Let's meet at 7, near the theater.

Coolgrl: See you then! Later!

Talk 🖑   Info ⚑   Send 📨

*T-G-I-F = Thank goodness it's Friday.

B Read the instant messages again. Check ☑ the statements that are true.

1. ☐ It's Friday.
2. ☐ Emily's not planning anything special.
3. ☐ It's not raining.
4. ☐ They're meeting at 7:00.
5. ☐ They're going to a play in the park.
6. ☐ They're eating lunch in the park.

C **GROUP WORK.** Walk around the class. Make plans to meet three classmates.

❝ What are you doing on Saturday? ❞

❝ I'm not doing anything special. Do you want to go to a movie? ❞

NEED HELP? **Here's language you already know:**

Events and places
a play   a party
a movie   a game
a concert   a speech

at the [stadium]
on the corner of [First Street]
    and [Main Street]
next to the [school]

Times and dates
on [Monday]
this weekend
in the evening
at [eight] o'clock

Questions
Would you like to go?
Do you want to get together?
Let's meet at [two thirty].

Weather expressions
It's [hot].
The weather is [beautiful].

D **WRITING.** On a separate piece of paper, write your plans for the next three days.

TOP NOTCH WEBSITE
For Unit 9 online activities, visit the *Top Notch* Companion Website at www.longman.com/topnotch.

UNIT WRAP-UP

- **Grammar.** Talk about the pictures. Use the present continuous.
  They're going to a concert. She's talking on the phone.

- **Social language.** Create conversations for the people.
  A: Let's meet later.
  B: OK. What time?

Thursday 6:30 P.M.

Concert
6:30 P.M.
Tonight

Saturday 9:00 A.M.

✔ **Now I can ...**

☐ describe today's weather.
☐ ask about people's activities.
☐ discuss plans.

83

UNIT 10

Food

UNIT GOALS

1 Get ingredients for a recipe
2 Offer and ask for foods at the table
3 Talk about present-time activities

LESSON 1

Get Ingredients for a Recipe

A 🎧 **VOCABULARY.** Foods: count nouns. Listen and practice.

1. an egg
2. an onion
3. an apple
4. an orange
5. a lemon
6. a banana
7. a tomato
8. a potato
9. a pepper
10. beans
11. peas

📖 **VOCABULARY BOOSTER** See pages V6 and V7 for more.

B 🎧 **LISTENING COMPREHENSION.** Listen to the conversations. Check ☑ the foods from the vocabulary you hear in each conversation. Then listen again to check your work.

1.	✔		✔			
2.						
3.						
4.						
5.						

C **GRAMMAR.** <u>How many</u> and <u>Are there any</u>

Use <u>How many</u> and <u>Are there any</u> with plural nouns.

How many tomatoes are there? Two.
How many peppers are there in the fridge? Four.
Are there any lemons in the fridge? Yes. There are three. / No, there aren't [any].

D 🎧 **VOCABULARY.** Places to keep food in a kitchen. **Listen and practice.**

1. **in the fridge** (*or* **in the refrigerator**)

2. **on the shelf**

3. **on the counter**

E **PAIR WORK.** Ask your partner questions about the pictures in Exercise D. Use **How many** and **Are there any**. Answer your partner's questions.

> ❝ Are there any beans in the fridge? ❞

> ❝ No, there aren't any. ❞

CONVERSATION • *Get ingredients for a recipe.*

1. 🎧 **MODEL.** Read and listen.

Wendy: How about some tomato potato soup?

Fred: Tomato potato? That sounds delicious! I love tomatoes and potatoes.

Wendy: Are there any potatoes on the shelf?

Fred: Yes, there are.

Wendy: And do we have any tomatoes?

Fred: I'll check.

2. 🎧 **Rhythm and intonation practice**

3. **PAIR WORK.** Role-play a conversation. Use the recipes. Start like this:

A: How about some _____?

B: _____? That sounds delicious! I love _____.

A: Are there any _____?

B: _____ . . .

Continue in your own way . . .

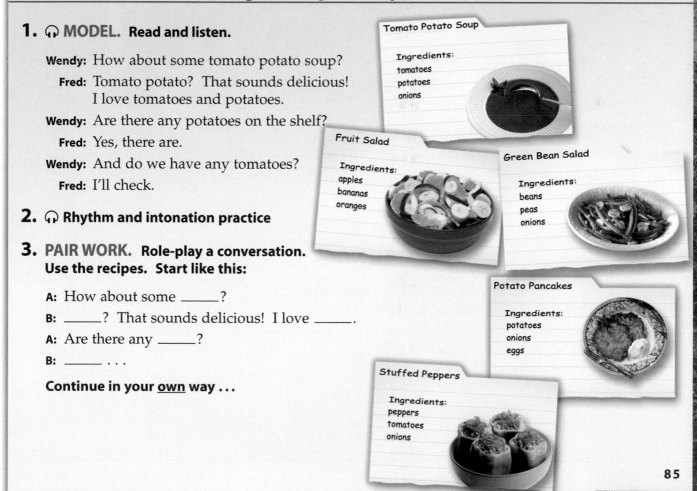

Tomato Potato Soup
Ingredients:
tomatoes
potatoes
onions

Fruit Salad
Ingredients:
apples
bananas
oranges

Green Bean Salad
Ingredients:
beans
peas
onions

Potato Pancakes
Ingredients:
potatoes
onions
eggs

Stuffed Peppers
Ingredients:
peppers
tomatoes
onions

Offer and Ask for Foods at the Table

A 🎧 **VOCABULARY.** Drinks and foods: non-count nouns. Listen and practice.

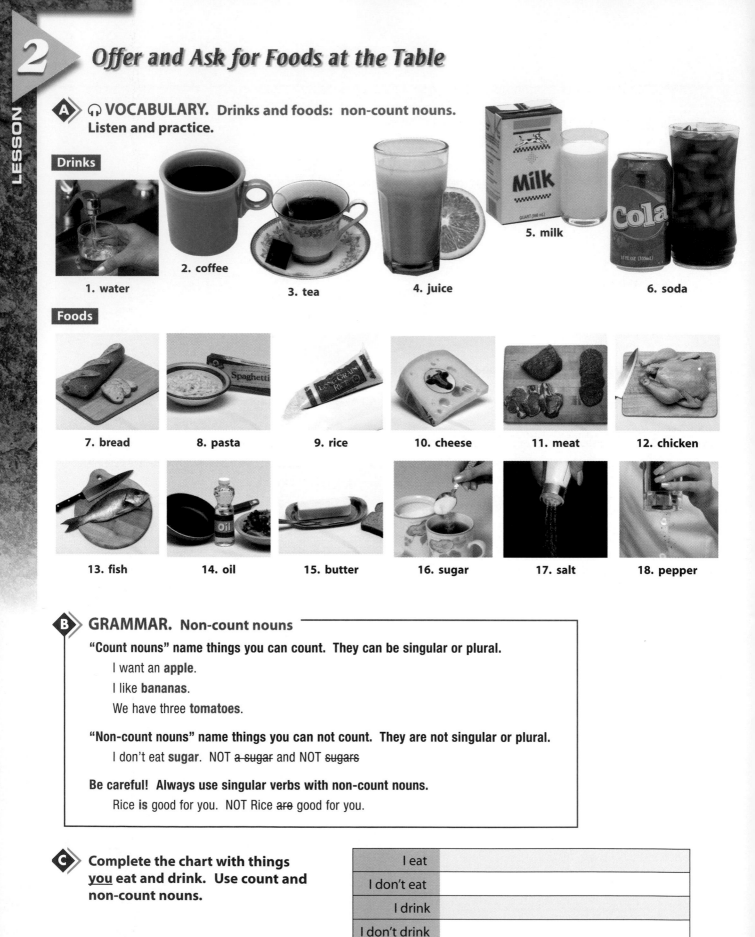

Drinks

1. water
2. coffee
3. tea
4. juice
5. milk
6. soda

Foods

7. bread
8. pasta
9. rice
10. cheese
11. meat
12. chicken

13. fish
14. oil
15. butter
16. sugar
17. salt
18. pepper

B **GRAMMAR.** Non-count nouns

"**Count nouns**" name things you can count. They can be singular or plural.

    I want an **apple**.
    I like **bananas**.
    We have three **tomatoes**.

"**Non-count nouns**" name things you can not count. They are not singular or plural.

    I don't eat **sugar**. NOT a~~sugar~~ and NOT ~~sugars~~

Be careful! Always use singular verbs with non-count nouns.

    Rice **is** good for you. NOT Rice ~~are~~ good for you.

C Complete the chart with things **you** eat and drink. Use count and non-count nouns.

I eat	
I don't eat	
I drink	
I don't drink	

D ▸ GRAMMAR. How much and Is there any

Use **How much** and **Is there any** with non-count nouns.
  How much sugar do you want?
  Is there any milk in the fridge?

But remember: Use **How many** and **Are there any** with plural count nouns.
  How many apples are there in the kitchen?
  Are there any bananas?

E ▸ 🎧 VOCABULARY. Containers and quantities. Listen and practice.

1. **a box** of pasta 2. **a loaf** of bread 3. **a bottle** of juice 4. **a can** of soup 5. **a bag** of onions

F ▸ Complete each question with How much or How many.

1. <u>How many</u> boxes of pasta are there in the kitchen?

2. _____ eggs are there in the fridge?

3. _____ rice is there on the shelf?

4. _____ bottles of juice are there on the shelf?

5. _____ sugar is in that coffee?

6. _____ cans of tomatoes do we have?

CONVERSATION • *Offer and ask for foods at the table.*

1. 🎧 **MODEL.** Read and listen.

Linda: Would you like coffee or tea?
Nicole: I'd like coffee, please. Thanks.
Linda: And would you like sugar?
Nicole: No, thanks.
Linda: Please pass the butter.
Nicole: Sure. Here you go.

2. 🎧 **Rhythm and intonation practice**

3. **PAIR WORK.** Role-play a conversation at the table. Use the guide, or create a new conversation.

A: Would you like _____ or _____?
B: I'd like _____, please. _____.
A: And would you like _____?
B: _____ . . .

Continue in your <u>own</u> way . . .

Talk about Present-time Activities

A **GRAMMAR.** The present continuous and the simple present tense

Use the present continuous for actions that continue in the present.
    He**'s eating** dinner now.
    We**'re studying** English this year.

Use the simple present tense for habitual actions.
    My husband **cooks** dinner for our family.
    I never **eat** eggs for breakfast. NOT I ~~am never eating~~ eggs for breakfast.

Use the simple present tense with <u>want</u>, <u>need</u>, and <u>like</u>.
    I **like** coffee. NOT I ~~am liking~~ coffee.

B **Complete each statement or question with the simple present tense or the present continuous.**

1. Who _____ lunch today?
   _{make}

2. We _____ any sugar.
   _{not need}

3. She sometimes _____ lunch early.
   _{eat}

4. They _____ milk in their coffee.
   _{not like}

5. I _____ the kitchen every day.
   _{clean}

6. I'm busy. I _____ the kids.
   _{feed}

7. What _____?
   _{Peter / need}

8. _____ onion soup?
   _{you / like}

9. What _____ now?
   _{they / do}

10. How much sugar _____ in your tea?
    _{you / want}

C **WRITING.** Look at the picture of Louisa Brown and her date book. On a separate piece of paper, write about Louisa. What is she doing right now? What does she do at other times? Use the present continuous and the simple present tense.

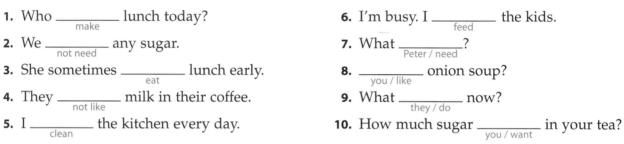

Louisa Brown

MAY 11

SCHEDULE

May	May
10 Monday Teach English [intermediate] at Linguatec: 10:00 A.M.	**Thursday 13** Work at home 8:00-12:00 Teach English [beginning] at Bank Street School: 4:00-6:00
11 Tuesday Work at home 8:00-12:00 Teach English [beginning] at Bank Street School: 4:00-6:00	**Friday 14** Study Chinese
12 Wednesday Teach English [intermediate] at Linguatec: 10:00 A.M.	**Saturday 15** Laundry / shopping **Sunday 16** Cook for Mom and Dad

Louisa is listening to music right now. On Mondays and Wednesdays, she teaches English at Linguatec.

D **PAIR WORK.** Write <u>yes</u> / <u>no</u> and information questions about Louisa. Use the present continuous and the simple present tense.

PRONUNCIATION. Vowel sounds. Listen and practice.

1. /i/	2. /ɪ/	3. /eɪ/	4. /ɛ/	5. /æ/
see	six	late	pepper	apple
tea	fish	potato	said	balcony
street	big	train	lemon	factory

CONVERSATION • *Invite someone to join you.*

1. **MODEL.** Read and listen.

Rita: Hey, Alison. Would you like to join me?

Alison: Sure. What are you drinking?

Rita: Lemonade.

Alison: Mmm. Sounds great. I think I'd like the same thing.

2. **Rhythm and intonation practice**

3. **PAIR WORK.** Role-play a conversation. **Use the guide, or create a new conversation.**

A: Hey, _____. Would you like to join me?

B: Sure. What are you _____?

A: _____.

B: Mmm. Sounds great. I think I'd like _____ . . .

Continue in your <u>own</u> way . . .

TOP NOTCH WEBSITE
For Unit 10 online activities, visit the *Top Notch* Companion Website at www.longman.com/topnotch.

A 🎧 **READING.** Read and listen to the two recipes.

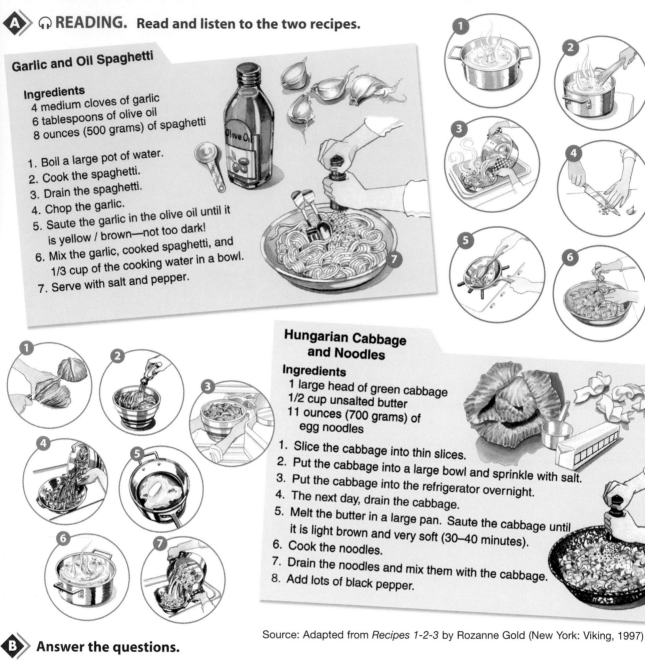

Garlic and Oil Spaghetti

Ingredients
4 medium cloves of garlic
6 tablespoons of olive oil
8 ounces (500 grams) of spaghetti

1. Boil a large pot of water.
2. Cook the spaghetti.
3. Drain the spaghetti.
4. Chop the garlic.
5. Saute the garlic in the olive oil until it is yellow / brown—not too dark!
6. Mix the garlic, cooked spaghetti, and 1/3 cup of the cooking water in a bowl.
7. Serve with salt and pepper.

Hungarian Cabbage and Noodles

Ingredients
1 large head of green cabbage
1/2 cup unsalted butter
11 ounces (700 grams) of egg noodles

1. Slice the cabbage into thin slices.
2. Put the cabbage into a large bowl and sprinkle with salt.
3. Put the cabbage into the refrigerator overnight.
4. The next day, drain the cabbage.
5. Melt the butter in a large pan. Saute the cabbage until it is light brown and very soft (30–40 minutes).
6. Cook the noodles.
7. Drain the noodles and mix them with the cabbage.
8. Add lots of black pepper.

Source: Adapted from *Recipes 1-2-3* by Rozanne Gold (New York: Viking, 1997)

B **Answer the questions.**

1. Are there any onions in the recipes? _____
2. Is there any pasta in the recipes? _____
3. Which recipe has butter? _____
4. Which recipe has garlic? _____

C **WHAT ABOUT YOU?** Create your <u>own</u> recipe with only three ingredients. Write the ingredients. Use a dictionary for the food names you don't know. Then tell the class about your recipe.

❝ My recipe is for my grandmother's chicken soup. It's very good… ❞

Name of food: _____
Ingredients:
_____
_____
_____

UNIT WRAP-UP

- **Vocabulary.** Look at the picture. Close your book. Write the names of all the foods and drinks you remember.

- **Grammar.** Ask questions about the picture. Use <u>How much</u>, <u>How many</u>, <u>Is there any</u>, and <u>Are there any</u>.
  A: How much pasta is there?   B: Four boxes.

- **Writing.** Write sentences about what the people are doing and their schedules.
  Michelle cleans the apartment on Mondays.

- **Social language.** Create conversations for Michelle and Peter.
  A: How about some potato pancakes?
  B: That sounds delicious.

SATURDAY

✔	Now I can ...
☐	get ingredients for a recipe.
☐	offer and ask for foods at the table.
☐	talk about present-time activities.

91

Past Events

UNIT GOALS

1 Talk about the past
2 Discuss past activities
3 Ask about a vacation

Talk about the Past

A 🎧 **VOCABULARY.** Past-time expressions. Listen and practice.

| 1. yesterday | today |

| 2. last { week month year Tuesday | today |

| 3. two { days weeks months years } ago | | today |

1998
4. nineteen ninety-eight

2000
5. two thousand

🎧 **How to say years**

1900	=	nineteen hundred
1901	=	nineteen oh one
2001	=	two thousand and one
2010	=	two thousand ten
1980–1989	=	the (nineteen) eighties
1901–2000	=	the twentieth century
2001–3000	=	the twenty-first century

B 🎧 **LISTENING COMPREHENSION. Listen to the years. Point to the year you hear.**

1967 1976
2001 2021

C **PAIR WORK. Now choose five years from the chart. Say a year to your partner. Your partner circles the year.**

2007	1907	1812
1940	1914	1900
1705	2017	1905
1805	1999	1919
2006	1814	1800

D **GRAMMAR. The past tense of be**

I
He } **was** at home last night.
She

It **was** cloudy yesterday.
She **wasn't** at work last Monday.

We
You } **were** colleagues in 1995.
They

There **were** a lot of people in the park this morning.
We **weren't** at the party last night.

Was Richard at school yesterday?

Where was his brother last night?

When was she in France?

Were your parents students in 1985?

Where were they two days ago?

When were you sick?

Contractions
was not → **wasn't**
were not → **weren't**

E Complete the sentences. Write <u>was</u> or <u>were</u>.

1. _____ she a student in 1995?

2. What _____ their address last year?

3. Where _____ Peter and Jen last week?

4. _____ there a party last night?

5. My parents _____ students in the seventies.

6. _____ his brothers at the park yesterday?

7. There _____ a lot of closets in her first house.

8. When _____ your father in Thailand?

F ⌒ **LISTENING COMPREHENSION.** **Listen to the conversations about events. Then listen again and circle the day or month.**

1. If today is Saturday, the party was on (Saturday / Friday / Thursday).

2. If this is May, then her birthday was in (June / April / March).

3. If today is Wednesday, the game was on (Monday / Tuesday / Sunday).

CONVERSATION • *Talk about the past.*

1. ⌒ **MODEL. Read and listen.**

Terri: Where were you last night?

Ruth: When?

Terri: At about 8:00.

Ruth: I was at home. Why?

Terri: There was a great party at the Pike Museum.

Ruth: There was? Too bad I wasn't there!

2. ⌒ **Rhythm and intonation practice**

3. **PAIR WORK.** Now role-play the conversation. Use the pictures and the guide, or create a new conversation.

A: Where were you _____?

B: When?

A: At _____.

B: I was _____. Why?

A: There was _____ at _____.

B: _____.

at the Drama School

at Smith Stadium

at Brown Park

93

Discuss Past Activities

A **GRAMMAR.** The simple past tense

Regular verbs

Add -ed to form the simple past tense. If the verb ends in -e, just add -d.

call → call**ed**   like → like**d**

I **called** my mother yesterday, but she wasn't home.

But remember:
study → stud**ied**
shop → shop**ped**

Irregular verbs

🎧 **Learn these irregular past tense forms.**

come → **came**	have → **had**	take → **took**
do → **did**	make → **made**	wake → **woke**
drive → **drove**	put → **put**	wear → **wore**
eat → **ate**	read → **read**	write → **wrote**
get → **got**	ride → **rode**	
go → **went**	see → **saw**	

To make negative statements, use didn't (did not) and the base form of a verb.

I **didn't go** to the movies last night. NOT I ~~didn't went~~ to the movies last night.

B 🎧 **PRONUNCIATION.** The simple past tense ending. **Listen and practice.**

1. /d/
played = play/d/
listened = listen/d/
exercised = exercise/d/

2. /t/
liked = like/t/
washed = wash/t/
shopped = shop/t/

3. /ɪd/
wanted = want/ɪd/
needed = need/ɪd/

C **Complete the postcard with the simple past tense form of the verbs.**

Dear Sally,
Greetings from San Francisco. I _____ a great
1. have
time yesterday. In the morning, I _____ to the
2. go
Museum of Modern Art. It _____ really great,
3. be
and I _____ the art a lot. For lunch, I _____ at
4. like   5. eat
a nice Italian restaurant called Little City. In the
afternoon, I _____ the cable car to Ghirardelli
6. take
Square. I _____ them make chocolate there.
7. watch
I _____ all over Fisherman's Wharf, and I
8. walk
_____ a lot of interesting people.
9. see

Thinking of you!
George

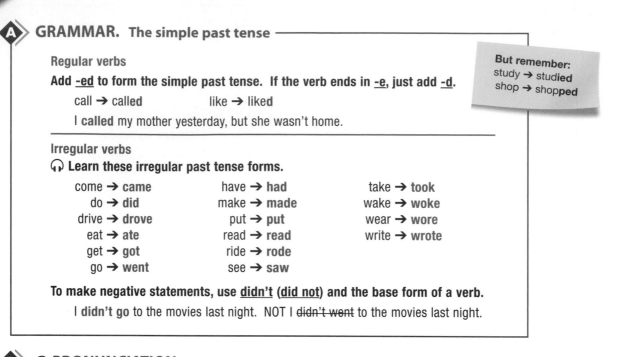

a cable car

Ghirardelli Chocolate

Fisherman's Wharf

D **WRITING.** On a separate piece of paper, write three things you
did yesterday. Write three things you didn't do. Then tell your
partner about your day.

❝I made dinner last night.
But I didn't wash the dishes.❞

VOCABULARY. Weekend activities.
Listen and practice.

1. **go to the beach**

2. **go running**

3. **go bike riding**

4. **go for a walk**

5. **go swimming**

6. **go for a drive**

📖 **VOCABULARY BOOSTER** See page V7 for more.

CONVERSATION • *Discuss past activities.*

1. 🎧 **MODEL.** **Read and listen.**

Hugo: Hi, Saul. How's it going?

Saul: Pretty good, thanks.

Hugo: What did you do last weekend?

Saul: Not much. I went running in the park on Saturday. What about you?

Hugo: About the same. I played soccer and went to a movie.

2. 🎧 **Rhythm and intonation practice**

3. PAIR WORK. Now exchange real information or use the pictures.

A: Hi, _____. How's it going?

B: _____.

A: What did you do _____?

B: Not much. I _____. What about you?

A: _____ . . .

Continue in your own way . . .

NEED HELP? Here's language you already know:

Past-time expressions
last week
last weekend
last month
last Friday

95

3 Ask about a Vacation

A 🎧 VOCABULARY. Seasons. Listen and practice.

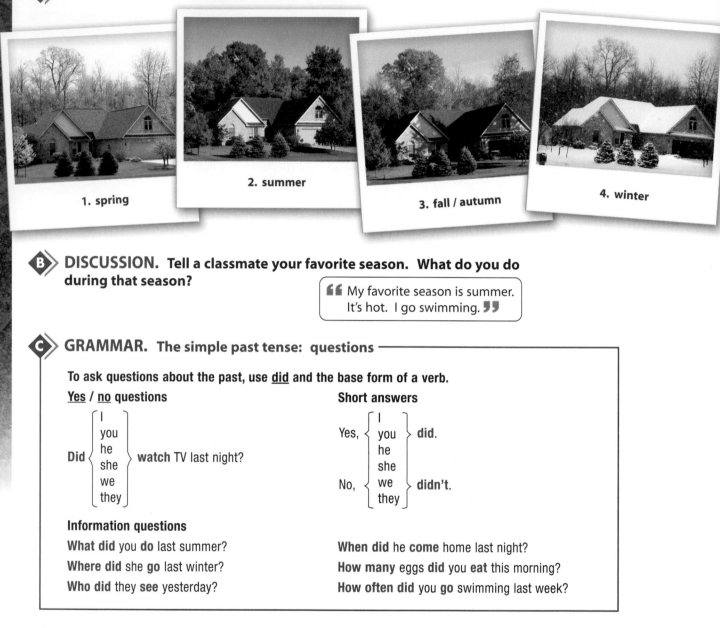

1. spring
2. summer
3. fall / autumn
4. winter

B DISCUSSION. Tell a classmate your favorite season. What do you do during that season?

> " My favorite season is summer.
> It's hot. I go swimming. "

C GRAMMAR. The simple past tense: questions

To ask questions about the past, use <u>did</u> and the base form of a verb.

<u>Yes</u> / <u>no</u> questions

Did { I / you / he / she / we / they } **watch** TV last night?

Short answers

Yes, { I / you / he / she } **did**.

No, { we / they } **didn't**.

Information questions

What did you **do** last summer?

Where did she **go** last winter?

Who did they **see** yesterday?

When did he **come** home last night?

How many eggs **did** you **eat** this morning?

How often did you **go** swimming last week?

D Complete the questions in the simple past tense.

1. **A:** _____ she _____ to the beach last summer?
   B: No, she went to her parents' house.

2. **A:** Where _____ they _____ dinner?
   B: They ate dinner at the Spring Street Cafe.

3. **A:** Who _____ she _____ last weekend?
   B: She saw her new classmate, Paul.

4. **A:** How often _____ he _____ bike riding?
   B: He went every day.

5. **A:** How many books _____ you _____?
   B: I read about three.

6. **A:** _____ you _____ the new restaurant?
   B: Yes, I really liked it.

CONVERSATION • *Ask about a vacation.*

1. ∩ **MODEL. Read and listen.**

Brian: You look great. Were you on vacation?

Naomi: Yes, I was. I just got back last week.

Brian: Where did you go?

Naomi: I went to London for two weeks.

Brian: No kidding. How was it?

Naomi: Really nice.

Brian: Well, it's great to see you. Welcome back.

Naomi: Thanks.

2. ∩ **Rhythm and intonation practice**

3. **PAIR WORK. Choose a vacation place. Use the photos or another place. Then role-play the conversation.**

A: You look _____. Were you on vacation?

B: _____. I just got back _____.

A: Where did you go?

B: _____.

A: _____. How was it?

B: _____ ...

Continue in your <u>own</u> way . . .

∩ **Positive and negative descriptions**

☺	☹
Really nice. Great. Wonderful.	Not good. Terrible. Awful.

Rio de Janeiro

Moscow

London

Rome

Hawaii

Istanbul

Hong Kong

TOP NOTCH
ACTIVITIES

A 🎧 **READING.** Read and listen. What's your dream vacation?

Where Did You Go on Vacation?

Luz Rodriguez

Last summer, my husband and I went to Paris for the first time. It was wonderful — we did so many things. Every night, we listened to music and went to bed late. And every morning, we got up late.

During the day, we walked the streets and visited tourist sites like the Eiffel Tower and the Louvre. We sat in cafes, drank coffee, and watched people. The food was great — we ate too much. I loved the bread and the cheese.

sunset in Cancun

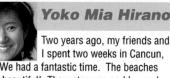
snorkeling

Tulum

John Barnes

My wife and I went to Hong Kong in 2003. What a great city! Every day, we went sightseeing. We took the ferry to Kowloon and looked at the beautiful views of the city. We went to Aberdeen and ate dinner on a boat. We visited the Tiger Balm Garden.

We mainly ate Chinese food, but sometimes we had Thai food or French food. The food in Hong Kong is terrific! My favorite was a dim sum restaurant that can serve 4800 people.

a Paris cafe

the Louvre

the Eiffel Tower

Yoko Mia Hirano

Two years ago, my friends and I spent two weeks in Cancun, Mexico. We had a fantastic time. The beaches were just beautiful! The water was so blue and warm.

Every morning we watched the sunrise, and in the evening we ate dinner on the beach and watched the sunset. The food was really good — the fish and fruit juices were very fresh. We went swimming right next to the ruins at Tulum. We took a water taxi to Isla Mujeres and went snorkeling. We saw so many beautiful fish!

a Hong Kong ferry

dim sum

Source: Authentic *Top Notch* interviews

B Answer the questions. Write sentences on a separate piece of paper.

1. Who went on vacation with her friends?
2. What did Luz Rodriguez do at night?
3. Who ate dinner on a boat?
4. What foods did Luz Rodriguez like?
5. How did John Barnes get to Kowloon?
6. What did Yoko Mia Hirano do in the evening?

C DISCUSSION. Where do **you** want to go on vacation?

❝ Me? I really want to go to Austria. ❞

D WRITING. On a separate piece of paper, write about a vacation that you took. Where did you go? What did you do? Then tell your class about your vacation.

I went to the beach last summer. Every day I . . .

🎧 **TOP NOTCH SONG**
"My Favorite Day"
Lyrics on last book page.

TOP NOTCH WEBSITE
For Unit 11 online activities, visit the *Top Notch* Companion Website at www.longman.com/topnotch.

- **Social language.** Create conversations for Don Baker and Karen Taylor. Ask about last weekend. Ask about a vacation.
  A: *What did you do last weekend?*
  B: *Not much. On Saturday I went shopping.*

- **Writing.** Choose Don or Karen. Write about what he or she did.
  Last Saturday Karen went shopping . . .

Last Saturday

Last Weekend

Last Vacation

Last Vacation

Now I can . . .

☐ talk about the past.
☐ discuss past activities.
☐ ask about a vacation.

99

Appearance and Health

UNIT GOALS

1 Describe people
2 Show concern about an injury
3 Suggest a remedy

LESSON 1

Describe People

A 🎧 VOCABULARY. Adjectives to describe hair. Listen and practice.

1. black   2. brown   3. red   4. blonde   5. gray   6. white

14. a mustache
15. a beard

7. dark   8. light

9. straight   10. wavy   11. curly   12. short   13. long

16. bald

B 🎧 LISTENING COMPREHENSION.
Listen to the descriptions of hair.
Write the number next to the picture.

C 🎧 VOCABULARY. The face.
Listen and practice.

8. brown eyes

9. blue eyes

10. green eyes

11. eyelashes

①

1. eye
2. eyebrow

4. ear

3. nose

5. mouth

7. neck

12. tooth

13. tongue

6. chin

one tooth → two **teeth**

D GRAMMAR. Use of adjectives for physical description

With be		**With have**
My eyes are blue.	OR	I have blue eyes.
Our hair is blonde.	OR	We have blonde hair.
Her eyelashes are long and dark.	OR	She has long, dark eyelashes.

E Complete the sentences with a form of be or have.

1. My sister's hair _____ long and wavy.
2. Paul's brother _____ curly, black hair.
3. My grandfather _____ a short, gray beard.
4. Her eyes _____ very beautiful.
5. Your sister's hair _____ so long!
6. We _____ straight, black hair.

CONVERSATION • *Describe people.*

1. 🎧 **MODEL. Read and listen.**

Max: Who's that? She looks familiar.

Diane: Who?

Max: The woman with long, curly, blonde hair.

Diane: Oh, that's Daniela Mercury. She's a singer from Brazil.

Max: No kidding!

2. 🎧 **Rhythm and intonation practice**

3. **PAIR WORK. Now talk about the people in the photos.**

A: Who's that? _____ looks familiar.

B: Who?

A: The _____ with _____.

B: Oh, that's _____. _____'s _____ from _____.

A: No kidding!

Daniela Mercury
singer (Brazil)

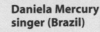

Andrea Bocelli
singer (Italy)

Chow Yun Fat
actor (Hong Kong)

Yao Ming
athlete (China)

Juliette Binoche
actress (France)

Luis Miguel
singer (Mexico)

Show Concern about an Injury

A 🎧 **VOCABULARY.** Parts of the body. Listen and practice.

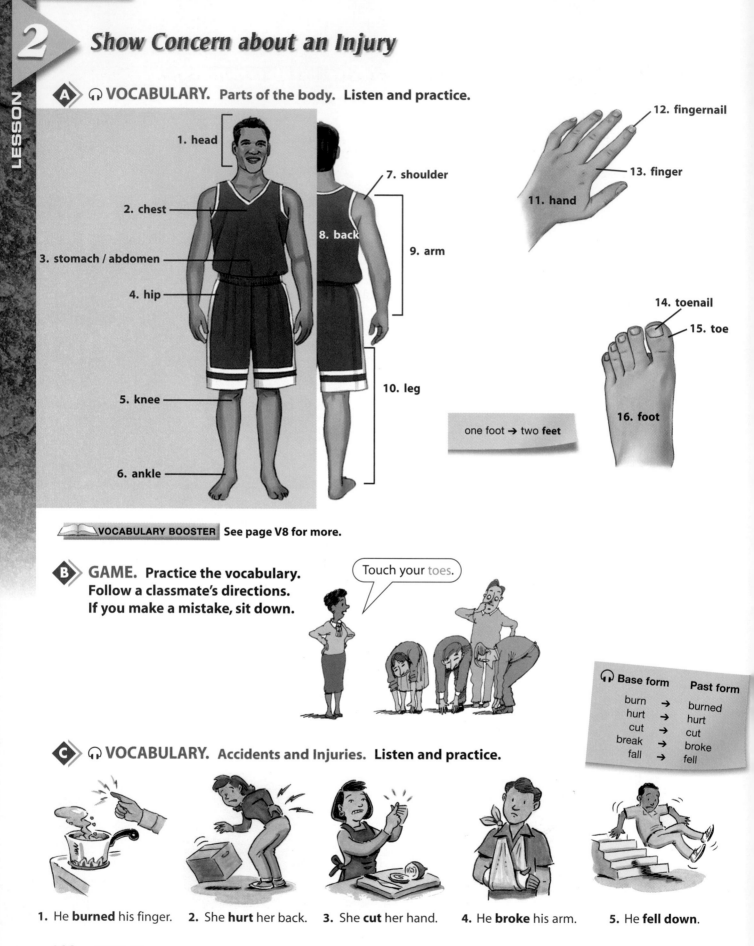

1. head
2. chest
3. stomach / abdomen
4. hip
5. knee
6. ankle
7. shoulder
8. back
9. arm
10. leg
11. hand
12. fingernail
13. finger
14. toenail
15. toe
16. foot

one foot → two **feet**

📖 **VOCABULARY BOOSTER** See page V8 for more.

B **GAME.** Practice the vocabulary. Follow a classmate's directions. If you make a mistake, sit down.

Touch your toes.

🎧 Base form		Past form
burn	→	burned
hurt	→	hurt
cut	→	cut
break	→	broke
fall	→	fell

C 🎧 **VOCABULARY.** Accidents and Injuries. Listen and practice.

1. He **burned** his finger.
2. She **hurt** her back.
3. She **cut** her hand.
4. He **broke** his arm.
5. He **fell down**.

D 🎧 **LISTENING COMPREHENSION.** **Listen. Write each injury. Then listen again to check your work.**

1. She ___burned her arm___ .

2. He _____ .

3. She _____ .

4. He _____ .

5. She _____ .

CONVERSATION • *Show concern about an injury.*

1. 🎧 **MODEL. Read and listen.**

Kate: Hey, Evan. What happened?

Evan: I broke my ankle.

Kate: I'm sorry to hear that.

2. 🎧 **Rhythm and intonation practice**

3. PAIR WORK. Now role-play the conversation. Use the pictures for ideas.

A: Hey, _____. What happened?

B: I _____.

A: I'm sorry to hear that.

103

Suggest a Remedy

A 🎧 **VOCABULARY. Ailments. Listen and practice.**

1. a headache   2. a stomachache   3. an earache   4. a backache   5. a toothache

6. a cold   7. a sore throat   8. a fever   9. a cough   10. a runny nose

B 🎧 **LISTENING COMPREHENSION. Listen to the conversations. Check ☑ the ailments.**

	a cold	a fever	a sore throat	a cough	a runny nose	a headache	a stomachache	a backache	a toothache
1.	☐	☐	☐	☐	☐	☐	☐	☐	☐
2.	☐	☐	☐	☐	☐	☐	☐	☐	☐
3.	☐	☐	☐	☐	☐	☐	☐	☐	☐
4.	☐	☐	☐	☐	☐	☐	☐	☐	☐
5.	☐	☐	☐	☐	☐	☐	☐	☐	☐
6.	☐	☐	☐	☐	☐	☐	☐	☐	☐

C 🎧 **VOCABULARY. Remedies. Listen and practice.**

1. take something   2. lie down   3. have some tea   4. see a doctor / dentist

D 🎧 **PRONUNCIATION. Back-vowel sounds. Listen and practice.**

1. /u/	2. /ʊ/	3. /oʊ/	4. /ɔ/	5. /ɑ/
tooth	foot	nose	cough	blonde
blue	good	toe	awful	hot
June	look	cold	daughter	doctor

E GRAMMAR. Should for advice

Ask for and give advice with **should** or **shouldn't** and the base form of a verb.

Questions
Should I **see** a doctor?
Should she **take** something?
What **should** she do?

Answers
Yes, you **should**.
No, she **shouldn't**.
She **should go** to bed.

I have a bad headache.

*You **should take** something.*

He has a fever.

*He **shouldn't go** to school today.*

F Suggest a remedy. Use **should** or **shouldn't** and the base form of a verb.

1. "I have a terrible backache."
   YOU ___You should lie down___.

2. "I don't feel so good. I think I have a fever."
   YOU _____.

3. "Oh, my mouth! What a toothache!"
   YOU _____.

4. "My mother has a bad cough."
   YOU _____.

5. "My son has a stomachache. He feels awful!"
   YOU _____.

6. "I feel terrible. I have a sore throat."
   YOU _____.

CONVERSATION • *Suggest a remedy.*

1. 🎧 **MODEL. Read and listen.**

Bill: I feel awful.
Sally: What's wrong?
Bill: I have a headache.
Sally: You really should take something.
Bill: Good idea.
Sally: I hope you feel better.

2. 🎧 **Rhythm and intonation practice**

3. PAIR WORK. Choose an ailment. Role-play suggesting a remedy for your partner. Use the guide, or create a new conversation.

B: I feel _____.
A: What's wrong?
B: _____.
A: You really _____.
B: _____.
A: I hope you feel better.

NEED HELP? **Here's language you already know:**

awful
terrible
bad

Good idea.
Thanks.
OK.

105

TOP NOTCH
ACTIVITIES

 A 🎧 **READING.** Look at the photos. Read and listen. Write the name of each person.

Gerard Depardieu
actor

Zhang Zi Yi
actress

Caetano Veloso
singer

Rob Reiner
film director

Julia Roberts
actress

1. She's very pretty. She has straight, black hair and brown eyes. She's wearing a red dress.
   name _____

4. He's handsome and has wavy, black hair. His eyes are brown. He's wearing a blue shirt.
   name _____

2. He's wearing a white shirt and a black jacket. He has brownish-blonde hair and blue eyes.
   name _____

5. She has long, red hair. She has pretty, brown eyes. She's wearing a black dress.
   name _____

3. He has blue eyes and a gray beard. His eyebrows are brown. He's bald. He's wearing a tie and a blue shirt.
   name _____

B **GUESSING GAME.** On a separate piece of paper, write a description of a classmate. Read your description to the class. The class guesses who it is.

> She's short and very good-looking. She has long hair and brown eyes. She's wearing a white blouse and a blue skirt.

TOP NOTCH WEBSITE
For Unit 12 online activities, visit the
Top Notch Companion Website at
www.longman.com/topnotch.

- **Vocabulary.** Make statements about the ailments and injuries in the picture.
  She has a cold.

- **Grammar.** Suggest remedies for the people in the picture.
  She should take something.

- **Social language.** Create conversations for the people.
  A: What happened?
  B: I fell down.

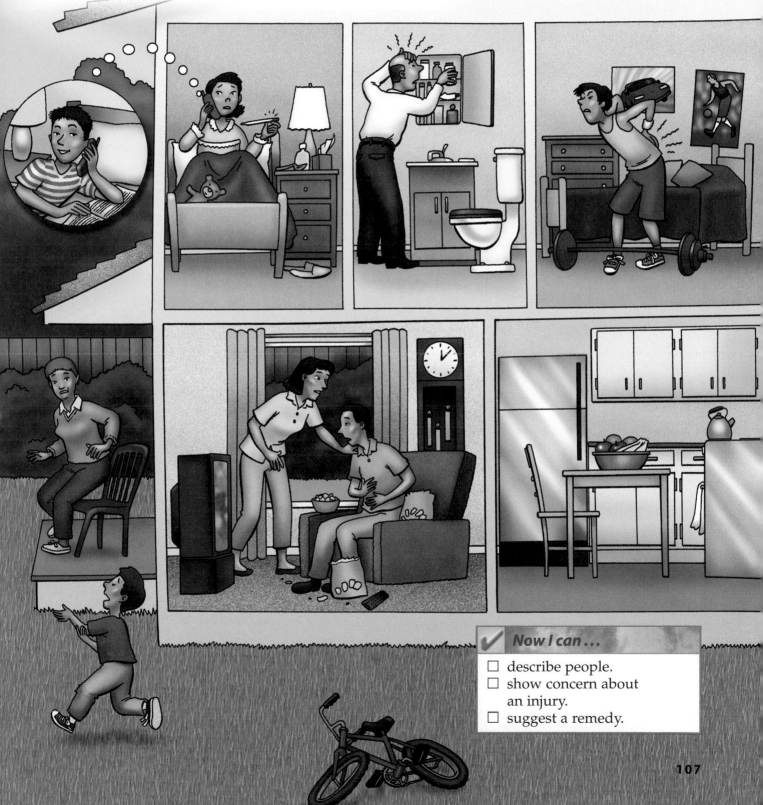

Now I can ...

- [ ] describe people.
- [ ] show concern about an injury.
- [ ] suggest a remedy.

UNIT 13

Abilities and Requests

UNIT GOALS

1 Discuss abilities
2 Decline an invitation
3 Request help or permission

1 Discuss Abilities

A **GRAMMAR.** <u>Can</u> and <u>can't</u>

To talk about ability, use <u>can</u> or <u>can't</u> and the base form of a verb.

She **can play** the guitar.   He **can't cook**.

Questions	Short answers
Can you **play** the guitar?	Yes, I **can**. / No, I **can't**.
Can he **speak** English?	Yes, he **can**. / No, he **can't**.

can not → **cannot** → **can't**

B 🎧 **PRONUNCIATION.** <u>Can</u> and <u>can't</u>. **Notice the pronunciation <u>and</u> stress. Listen and practice.**

/kən/   /kænt/

1. I can play the guitar.   I can't play the piano.
2. I can speak English.   I can't speak Italian.
3. I can make pasta.   I can't make soup.

C 🎧 **VOCABULARY.** Abilities and skills. **Listen and practice.**

1. sew   2. knit   3. paint   4. draw   5. dance

6. swim   7. drive   8. play the violin   9. ski   10. fix a car

📖 **VOCABULARY BOOSTER** See page V8 for more.

D Check ☑ the things <u>you</u> can do. Then tell your class about yourself.

❝I can't play the guitar, but I can sing.❞

I can:	☐ sew	☐ drive	☐ fix a car	☐ ski
	☐ knit	☐ sing	☐ paint	☐ cook
	☐ dance	☐ play the guitar	☐ draw	☐ swim

E 🎧 **VOCABULARY.** Adverbs to describe ability. Listen and practice.

1. Tom sings ⎰ **well.**
⎱ **beautifully.**
⎰ **nicely.**

2. Ryan sings ⎰ **badly.**
⎱ **poorly.**
⎰ **terribly.**

> **Be careful!**
> He speaks English well.
> NOT ~~He speaks well English.~~

F Complete the conversations with <u>can</u> or <u>can't</u> and the base form of a verb.

1. **A:** _____ you _____ a car?
   B: Yes, I _____. But I don't drive well.

2. **A:** _____ John _____ well?
   B: Yes, he _____. He swims nicely.

3. **A:** _____ your brother _____?
   B: No. He _____ cook at all.

4. **A:** _____ Gloria _____ English well?
   B: Yes. She speaks English well.

5. **A:** _____ your grandmother _____?
   B: Yes. She knits beautifully.

6. **A:** _____ you _____ the guitar?
   B: No, I _____. I play very badly.

CONVERSATION • *Discuss abilities.*

1. 🎧 **MODEL. Read and listen.**

Gene: Can you swim?
Amy: No. Can you?
Gene: Yes. I swim very well.
Amy: When did you learn?
Gene: When I was about eight.
Amy: Was it hard?
Gene: Not at all!

2. 🎧 **Rhythm and intonation practice**

3. **PAIR WORK.** Now exchange real information.

A: Can you _____?
B: _____. Can you?
A: _____ . . .

Continue in your <u>own</u> way . . .

Decline an Invitation

A GRAMMAR. Too + adjective

Use **too** with an adjective to express a problem.

I can't drink this tea.
It's **too hot**.

I don't want those shoes.
They're **too expensive**.

I can't read.
I'm **too tired**.

B Write sentences with **too** and an adjective.

1. I can't eat this soup.

    It's too hot .

2. She can't buy those shoes.

_____.

3. I don't want this sofa.

_____.

4. She can't wear those pants.

_____.

5. He doesn't want that shirt.

_____.

6. She can't go swimming today.

_____.

VOCABULARY. Reasons to decline an invitation. Listen and practice.

1. I'm too busy.

2. I don't feel well.

3. It's too late.

4. I have other plans.

CONVERSATION • *Decline an invitation.*

1. **MODEL.** **Read and listen.**

Carl: Let's go to the movies.

Lucy: I'm really sorry. I'm too busy.

Carl: That's too bad. Maybe some other time.

2. **Rhythm and intonation practice**

3. PAIR WORK. Suggest an activity. Decline the invitation. Use the photos or other places and events.

A: Let's _____.

B: I'm really sorry. _____.

A: _____. Maybe some other time.

111

Request Help or Permission

A 🎧 **VOCABULARY.** Could you please . . . ? **Listen and practice.**

1. Could you please open the window?

2. Could you please close the door?

3. Could you please turn on the light?

4. Could you please turn off the TV?

5. Could you please help me?

6. Could you please hand me my glasses?

B 🎧 **LISTENING COMPREHENSION.** **Listen to the requests. Write the number on the correct picture. Then listen again to check your work.**

C ▷ GRAMMAR. Requests with Could or Can

Use questions with <u>Could you</u> or <u>Can you</u> and the base form of a verb to make requests.

Could you turn on the light? OR **Can you** turn on the light?

Use <u>please</u> to make a request more polite.

Could you **please** help me? OR Can you **please** help me?

Use questions with <u>can</u> or <u>could</u> and the base form to ask for permission.

Can I please open the window?	Sure. No problem.
Could we watch TV?	No, not now. Sorry.

D ▷ Complete the polite requests for help or permission. Use <u>please</u>.

1. After dinner, _could you please wash_ the dishes?

2. I'm so cold. _____ the window?

3. _____ the laundry this afternoon?

4. _____ the garbage tonight?

5. It's so windy. _____ the door?

6. _____ lunch? I'm too busy!

CONVERSATION • *Request help.*

1. ⌕ **MODEL.** Read and listen.

Tina: Could you do me a favor?

Roger: Sure. What?

Tina: Could you please close the window?

Roger: No problem.

2. ⌕ **Rhythm and intonation practice**

3. PAIR WORK. Now ask your partner to do you a favor.

A: Could you do me a favor?

B: _____. What?

A: Could you please _____?

B: _____.

NEED HELP? **Here's language you already know:**

Possible responses
Sure. No problem.
Sorry, I can't. I'm too busy.

TOP NOTCH
ACTIVITIES

TOP NOTCH WEBSITE
For Unit 13 online activities, visit the
Top Notch Companion Website at
www.longman.com/topnotch.

A ⌂ **READING.** Read and listen.

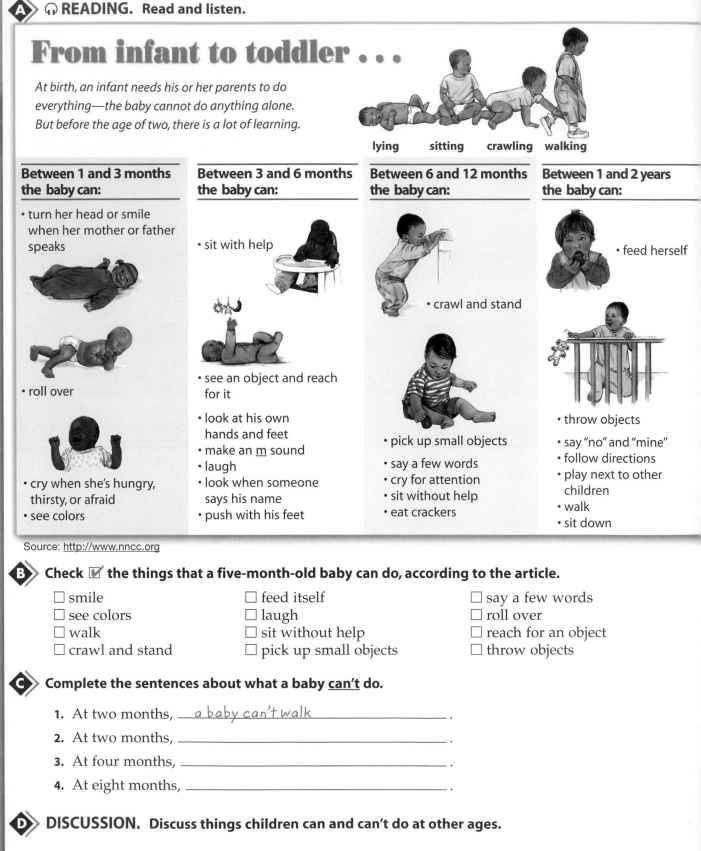

From infant to toddler . . .

*At birth, an infant needs his or her parents to do
everything—the baby cannot do anything alone.
But before the age of two, there is a lot of learning.*

lying   sitting   crawling   walking

**Between 1 and 3 months
the baby can:**

• turn her head or smile
when her mother or father
speaks

• roll over

• cry when she's hungry,
thirsty, or afraid
• see colors

**Between 3 and 6 months
the baby can:**

• sit with help

• see an object and reach
for it
• look at his own
hands and feet
• make an <u>m</u> sound
• laugh
• look when someone
says his name
• push with his feet

**Between 6 and 12 months
the baby can:**

• crawl and stand

• pick up small objects

• say a few words
• cry for attention
• sit without help
• eat crackers

**Between 1 and 2 years
the baby can:**

• feed herself

• throw objects
• say "no" and "mine"
• follow directions
• play next to other
children
• walk
• sit down

Source: http://www.nncc.org

B Check ☑ the things that a five-month-old baby can do, according to the article.

☐ smile   ☐ feed itself   ☐ say a few words
☐ see colors   ☐ laugh   ☐ roll over
☐ walk   ☐ sit without help   ☐ reach for an object
☐ crawl and stand   ☐ pick up small objects   ☐ throw objects

C Complete the sentences about what a baby <u>can't</u> do.

1. At two months, ___*a baby can't walk*___ .

2. At two months, _____ .

3. At four months, _____ .

4. At eight months, _____ .

D **DISCUSSION.** Discuss things children can and can't do at other ages.

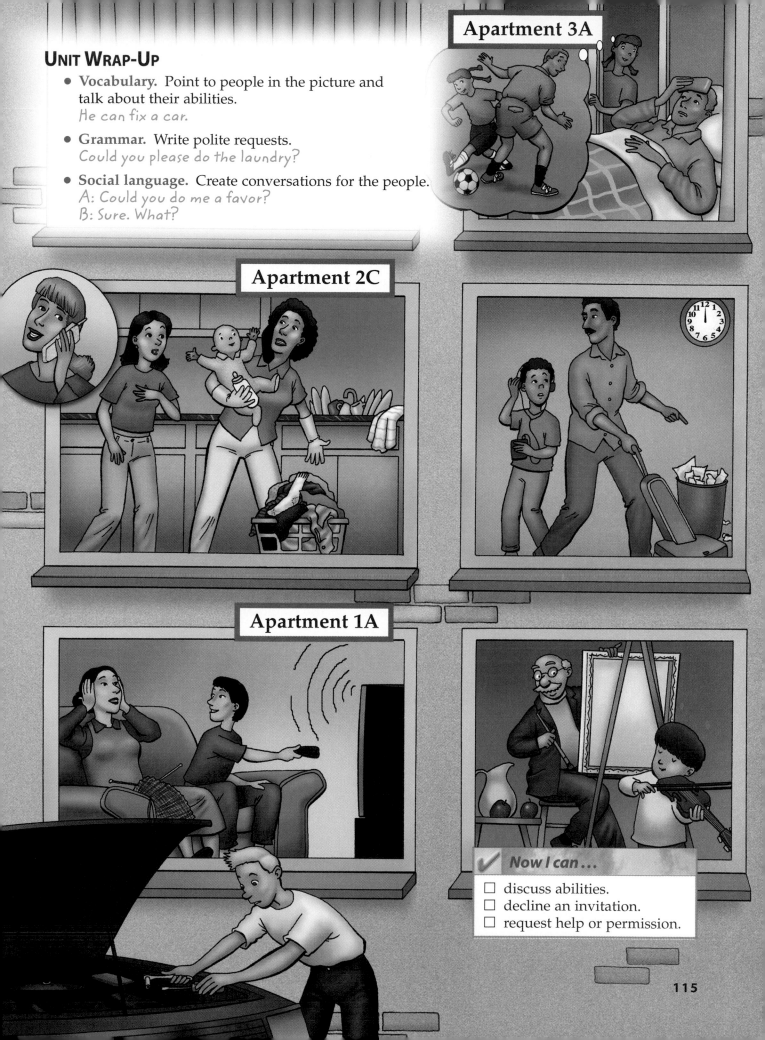

UNIT WRAP-UP

- **Vocabulary.** Point to people in the picture and talk about their abilities.
  He can fix a car.

- **Grammar.** Write polite requests.
  Could you please do the laundry?

- **Social language.** Create conversations for the people.
  A: Could you do me a favor?
  B: Sure. What?

Apartment 3A

Apartment 2C

Apartment 1A

✔ Now I can...

☐ discuss abilities.
☐ decline an invitation.
☐ request help or permission.

UNIT 14

UNIT GOALS

1 Get to know someone's life story
2 Announce good news and bad news
3 Ask about free-time activities

Past, Present, and Future Plans

1 **LESSON**

Get to Know Someone's Life Story

A 🎧 **VOCABULARY. Birth and childhood. Listen and practice.**

1. be born

2. grow up

3. go to school

4. move

5. study

6. graduate

B 🎧 **LISTENING COMPREHENSION.   Listen to the conversation about Miyuki Sato's life. Then listen again and check ✓ the statements that are true.**

1. ☐ Miyuki Sato was born in Japan.
2. ☐ Her father worked in Peru.
3. ☐ She grew up in Peru.
4. ☐ Miyuki speaks Chinese.
5. ☐ The family never moved to Japan.

C **PAIR WORK.   Interview your partner. Write the answers.**

1. When were you born? _____
2. Where were you born? _____
3. Where did you grow up? _____

D 🎧 **PRONUNCIATION. Diphthongs. Listen and practice.**

1. /aɪ/
die
I
time
tie

2. /aʊ/
how
house
noun
town

3. /ɔɪ/
boy
Roy
oil
boil

E 🎧 **VOCABULARY.** Academic subjects.
Listen and practice.

1. architecture

2. medicine

3. psychology

4. business

5. education

6. mathematics / math

7. science

8. nursing

9. engineering

10. law

📖 **VOCABULARY BOOSTER** See page V9 for more.

CONVERSATION • *Get to know someone's life story.*

1. 🎧 **MODEL. Read and listen.**

Elena: Where were you born?

Sam: In New York.

Elena: And did you grow up there?

Sam: Yes, I did. And you?

Elena: I was born in Brasilia.
I grew up in Toronto.

Sam: Toronto? That's interesting.
Why did you move there?

Elena: My parents are Canadian.

2. 🎧 **Rhythm and intonation practice**

3. PAIR WORK. Now exchange real information. Start like this:

A: Where were you born?

B: In _____.

Continue in your <u>own</u> way . . .

NEED HELP? **Here's language you already know:**

What do you do?
What are you studying now?
Where did you study?
Did you graduate?
What did you study?

Announce Good News and Bad News

A 🎧 **VOCABULARY.** More life events. Listen and practice.

1. get married
2. get divorced
3. have children
4. live happily ever after
5. die

B **GRAMMAR.** Would like

She **would like to have** two children.
I'd like to study architecture.

I would like → **I'd like**

Would you **like to have** children?　Yes, **I would.** / No, **I wouldn't.**
What **would** he **like to study**?　Chinese.

C **WHAT ABOUT YOU?** Complete the survey. Then, on a separate piece of paper, write statements with <u>would like</u>.

I'd like to have children in the next two years.

What would you like to do in the next two years?

☐ get married
☐ graduate
☐ have children
☐ move to a new country
☐ move to a new city

☐ move to a new apartment or house
☐ study a new language
☐ write a book
☐ learn to play a musical instrument
☐ get a new boss

☐ meet a good-looking man
☐ meet a good-looking woman
☐ meet a Scorpio
☐ paint my living room
☐ buy a new refrigerator

Scoring: Give yourself 1 point for each check mark.
0-5 points: Time to do something new!
6-10 points: Wow! Sounds like you have an interesting life.
11-15 points: Relax! You're going to do too much.

MYSELF Magazine

D **PAIR WORK.** Compare your survey with a partner's.

GRAMMAR. <u>Be going to</u> for the future

Next year, I**'m going to have** a baby.
He**'s going to move** to Italy.

Are you **going to study** architecture?   Yes, I am. / No, I'm not.
Who**'s going to graduate** tomorrow?   Jeannette.
When **are** you **going to have** children?   I don't know.

F **Write questions or statements with <u>be going to</u>.**

1. Where / you study ___*Where are you going to study*___?

2. My sister / have a baby / in September _____.

3. When / they get married _____?

4. My neighbor / get divorced _____.

5. My brother and I / study medicine _____.

CONVERSATION • *Announce good news and bad news.*

1. 🎧 **MODEL. Read and listen.**

Tom: Hi, Scott. What's new?

Scott: Well, I have some great news.
My daughter is going to have a baby.

Tom: Congratulations!

Scott: Thanks.

2. 🎧 **Rhythm and intonation practice**

3. PAIR WORK. Now role-play a conversation about good news or bad news.

A: Hi, _____. What's new?

B: Well, I have some _____ news. _____.

A: _____ . . .

Continue in your <u>own</u> way . . .

🎧 **Responses to good news**
• Congratulations!
• I'm so happy for you.
• I'm so happy to hear that.
• Best wishes!

🎧 **Responses to bad news**
• I'm sorry.
• Oh no. I'm sorry.
• I'm so sorry to hear that.
• That's too bad. I'm so sorry.

Ask about Free-time Activities

A ⌒ **VOCABULARY.** Free-time activities. **Listen and practice.**

1. travel   2. go camping   3. go fishing   4. relax

5. hang out with friends   6. sleep late   7. do nothing

Also remember
- exercise • paint
- go running • read
- go to the beach

📖 **VOCABULARY BOOSTER** See page V9 for more.

B ⌒ **LISTENING COMPREHENSION. Listen. Complete each statement.
Then listen again to check your work.**

1. He's going to ___go camping___.

2. She's going to _____.

3. They're going to _____.

4. She's going to _____.

5. He's going to _____.

6. He's going to _____.

C **GRAMMAR. Conditions and results in the future** ─────────

if- clause [condition]	future result
If the weather **is** nice,	**I'm going to go** to the beach.
If the weather **isn't** nice,	**I'm going to sleep** late.

Always use the present tense in the if- clause.

    If she **has** enough time, she's going to see the movie again. NOT If she ~~is going to have~~ enough time . . .

An if- clause can come at the beginning of the sentence or at the end.

    If **she stays home**, she's going to relax. OR She's going to relax **if she stays home**.

D **Complete the conditional sentences.**

1. If we _____ enough money, we're going to travel this summer.
   <u>have / are having</u>

2. If there is enough time, they _____ a vacation.
   <u>take / are going to take</u>

3. If Mark _____ his ticket today, the concert is going to be very expensive.
   <u>doesn't buy / isn't buying</u>

4. If Carla and Ed _____ married, they're going to have lots of children.
   <u>are going to get / get</u>

5. She _____ to Paris if she gets divorced.
   <u>'s going to move / moves</u>

6. If you don't leave now, you _____ late.
   <u>'re going to be / are</u>

7. I'm not going to clean the house tomorrow if it _____ too hot.
   <u>going to be / is</u>

8. What are you going to do if you _____ enough time this summer?
   <u>have / having</u>

E **PAIR WORK.** **Ask and answer the following questions. Then, on a separate piece of paper, write about your partner.**

1. If the weather is nice this weekend, what are you going to do?

2. If you have enough time today, what are you going to do?

3. If you have enough money, where are you going to go?

CONVERSATION • *Ask about free-time activities.*

1. ⌒ **MODEL. Read and listen.**

Pam: What do you like to do in your free time?

Katy: Well, I like to hang out with friends.

Pam: So, are you going to do that this weekend?

Katy: Maybe.

3. PAIR WORK. Now make small talk with your partner. Use the pictures for ideas.

A: What do you like to do in your free time?

B: Well, I like to _____.

A: So, are you going to do that _____?

B: _____.

2. ⌒ **Rhythm and intonation practice**

TOP NOTCH SONG
"I Wasn't Born Yesterday"
Lyrics on last book page.

TOP NOTCH WEBSITE
For Unit 14 online activities, visit the
Top Notch Companion Website at
www.longman.com/topnotch.

A ∩ **READING.** Read and listen to the article.
Then answer the questions.

Thor Heyerdahl, Explorer

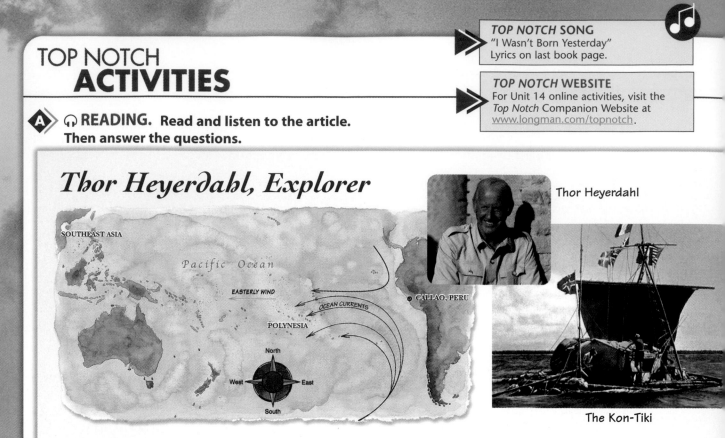

Thor Heyerdahl

The Kon-Tiki

Thor Heyerdahl was born in Norway in 1914. Heyerdahl got married in 1937. He and his wife, Liv, moved to Polynesia that year. While they lived there, Heyerdahl liked to go fishing. When he went fishing, he studied the wind and the Pacific Ocean currents.

In 1947, people thought that the first Polynesians had come from the west, from Southeast Asia. Because of the winds and the ocean currents, Heyerdahl had a different idea.

He thought the first Polynesians had come from the east.

In 1947, Heyerdahl made the Kon-Tiki, a raft of balsa wood. With a crew of men from many countries, he traveled 8000 kilometers [4300 miles] from Callao, Peru, to Polynesia. The voyage of the Kon-Tiki was very difficult. It took 101 days. But it proved that Heyerdahl's idea was possible. Heyerdahl died in 2002.

Information source: *Kon-Tiki: Across the Pacific by Raft* by Thor Heyerdahl (New York: Pocket Books, 1990)

1. What was Heyerdahl's occupation? *Thor Heyerdahl was an explorer* .

2. Where was he from? _____ .

3. When was he born? _____ .

4. When did he get married? _____ .

5. What was his wife's name? _____ .

6. Where did he move in 1937? _____ .

7. What did he study? _____ .

8. Where did he travel to in 1947? _____ .

9. **Challenge:** Why did Heyerdahl build the Kon-Tiki? _____ .

B **WHAT ABOUT YOU?** On a separate piece of paper, write a short history of **your** life. Include a picture. Then tell your class about it.

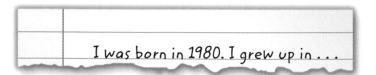

I was born in 1980. I grew up in . . .

- Tell the story of Katherine Rudy's life in the past, present, and future. What did she do? What is she doing now? What would she like to do?

  Katherine was born in 1981. She grew up in Chicago . . .

June 24, 1981 Seattle, Washington

Katherine Rudy
baby girl
born 6/24

June 24, 1991 Chicago, Illinois

33 Riverside Drive

May 30, 2001 Tampa, Florida

Congratulations, 2001 Graduates
Baker University of Science

Today

CHEMCARE LABS

Kemper

K. Rudy

Future

Katherine & Peter
JUST MARRIED

Future

Now I can...

☐ get to know someone's life story.
☐ announce good news and bad news.
☐ ask about free-time activities.

A 🎧 **LISTENING COMPREHENSION.** Listen to the conversations and check ☑ each statement __True__ or __False__. Then listen again to check your work.

	True	False
1. She likes soup for breakfast.	☐	☐
2. She gets up early every day.	☐	☐
3. He makes the beds.	☐	☐
4. He often takes a nap.	☐	☐
5. She gets dressed before breakfast.	☐	☐
6. He takes the bus to work.	☐	☐

B Write a sentence about each picture. Use the present continuous.

1. _She's getting up_ .

4. _____ .

2. _____ .

5. _____ .

3. _____ .

6. _____ .

C ▸ PAIR WORK. Write questions about daily activities. Use <u>When</u>, <u>What time</u>, <u>How often</u>, and <u>Who</u>. Ask your partner the questions. Write your partner's answers.

Questions	Your partner's answers
What time do you get up ?	_7:00_ .
1. _____ ?	_____ .
2. _____ ?	_____ .
3. _____ ?	_____ .
4. _____ ?	_____ .

D ▸ GROUP WORK. Tell the class about your partner's daily activities.

> 🙶 Jack gets up at 7:00 every day. 🙶🙶

E ▸ Complete each sentence with the simple present tense of the verb.

Let me tell you about life in my family. We all _____ at about 6:00. But
                                     1. get up
after that, everyone _____ a different routine. My mom _____ to work early,
                 2. have   3. go
and she _____ time for breakfast. So she _____ a quick cup of coffee and
        4. [not] have   5. drink
_____ out the door. My father _____ at home. He _____ breakfast for the
6. run   7. work   8. make
family. He _____ into the kitchen at about 6:15 and _____ to music as
       9. go   10. listen
he _____ breakfast. After breakfast, my sisters _____ the school bus, but I
  11. cook   12. take
_____ a little more time. I _____ the breakfast dishes, _____ my teeth, _____
13. have   14. wash   15. brush   16. comb
my hair, and then I _____ to school. On Saturdays, my mom _____ the house,
              17. walk   18. clean
and my dad _____ the laundry. On the weekend, we make our beds in the
       19. do
morning. From Monday to Friday, we _____ time to make our beds.
                            20. [not] have

PAIR WORK • *Exchange real information about your typical day.*

Start like this: What's your typical week like?

💡 **Ideas**

Talk about:
• household chores
• daily activities
• weekdays / weekends

F Write the present participle of each of the following verbs.

1. write ___writing___
2. make _____
3. wear _____
4. watch _____
5. shop _____

6. get up _____
7. have _____
8. do _____
9. drive _____
10. study _____

G Write the activity. Use the present continuous.

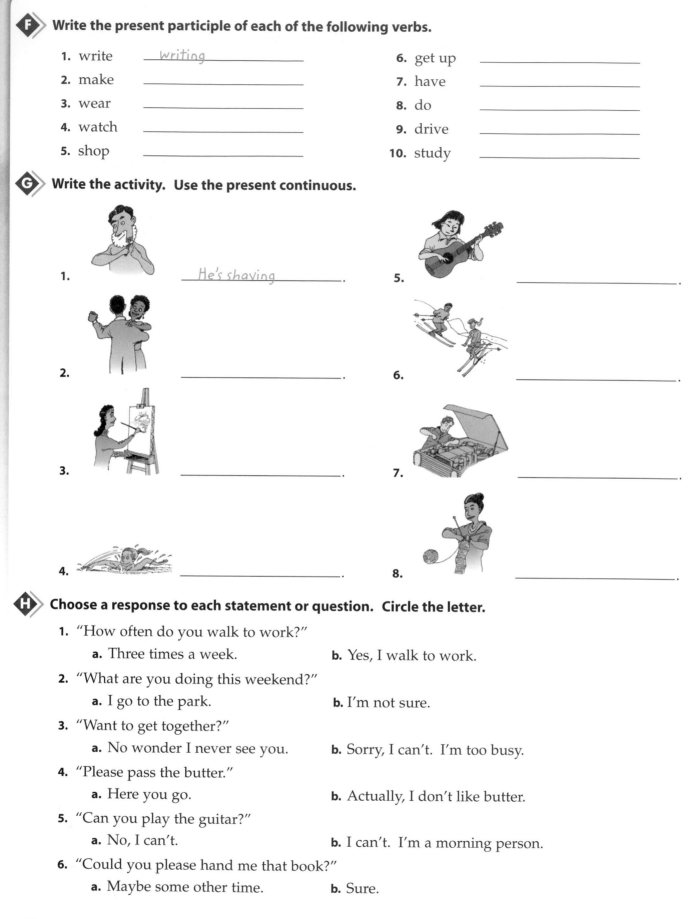

1. ___He's shaving___.

5. _____.

2. _____.

6. _____.

3. _____.

7. _____.

4. _____.

8. _____.

H Choose a response to each statement or question. Circle the letter.

1. "How often do you walk to work?"
   a. Three times a week.
   b. Yes, I walk to work.

2. "What are you doing this weekend?"
   a. I go to the park.
   b. I'm not sure.

3. "Want to get together?"
   a. No wonder I never see you.
   b. Sorry, I can't. I'm too busy.

4. "Please pass the butter."
   a. Here you go.
   b. Actually, I don't like butter.

5. "Can you play the guitar?"
   a. No, I can't.
   b. I can't. I'm a morning person.

6. "Could you please hand me that book?"
   a. Maybe some other time.
   b. Sure.

7. "My daughter's going to get married."

    a. I'm sorry. I'm too busy.   **b.** That's great!

8. "Should I call you back later?"

    a. Yes, please. I'm feeding the kids.   **b.** I can't. I'm making lunch.

9. "What's wrong?"

    a. I have a terrible cold.   **b.** You should take something.

PAIR WORK. **Write your <u>own</u> response to each statement or question. Then practice your exchanges with a partner.**

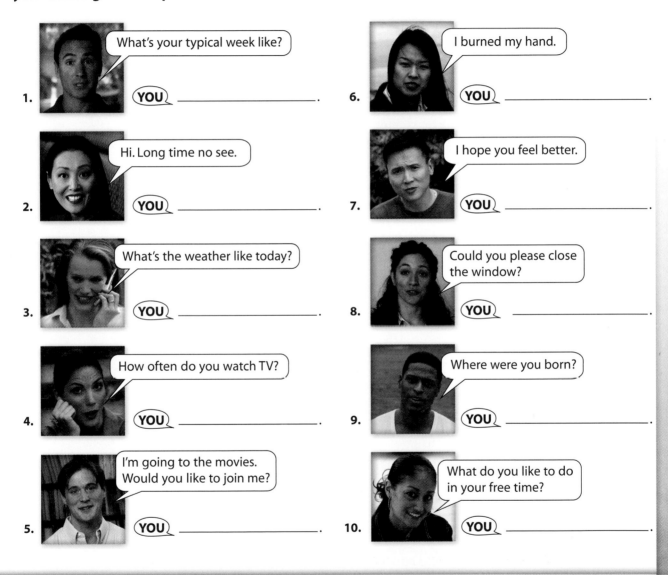

1. What's your typical week like? — YOU _____.

2. Hi. Long time no see. — YOU _____.

3. What's the weather like today? — YOU _____.

4. How often do you watch TV? — YOU _____.

5. I'm going to the movies. Would you like to join me? — YOU _____.

6. I burned my hand. — YOU _____.

7. I hope you feel better. — YOU _____.

8. Could you please close the window? — YOU _____.

9. Where were you born? — YOU _____.

10. What do you like to do in your free time? — YOU _____.

PAIR WORK • *Exchange real information about your life.*

💡 *Ideas*

Ask:
- When were you born?
- Where were you born?
- Where did you grow up?
- What did you study? OR What are you studying now?

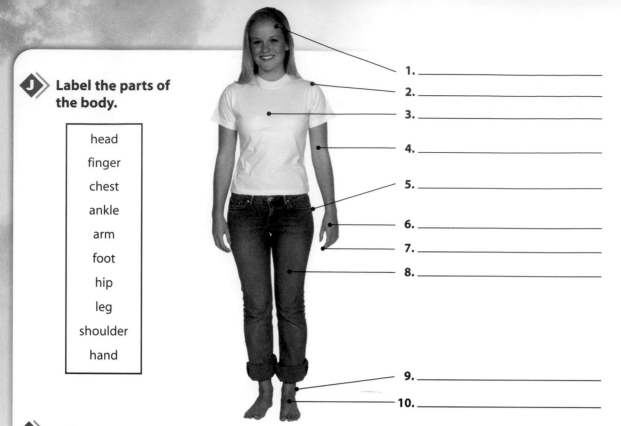

J **Label the parts of the body.**

| head |
| finger |
| chest |
| ankle |
| arm |
| foot |
| hip |
| leg |
| shoulder |
| hand |

1. _____
2. _____
3. _____
4. _____
5. _____
6. _____
7. _____
8. _____
9. _____
10. _____

K **Write statements and questions about the future. Use <u>be going to</u>.**

1. This weekend / they / see a great movie <u>*This weekend they're going to see a great movie*</u> .
2. When / you / make the beds _____?
3. What / he / study _____?
4. I / have / four children _____.
5. you / take a vacation this summer _____?

L **Underline the base form of the verb in the following sentences.**

1. I can <u>write</u> English but I can't <u>speak</u> English.
2. Do you like coffee for breakfast?
3. What do you do?
4. I'm going to take a nap.

5. They can't go to the train station at 3:00.
6. You should see a doctor.
7. Could you please open the door?
8. He shouldn't go to work today.

M **Write the name of each container.**

1.  a _____ of soda

2.  a _____ of tea

3. 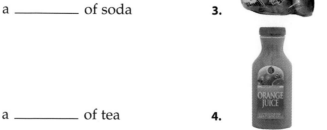 a _____ of potatoes

4. a _____ of juice

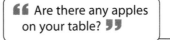
" Are there any apples on your table? "

" No, there aren't. "

 PAIR WORK. Look at the pictures.
Ask your partner questions about his or her table.

PARTNER A

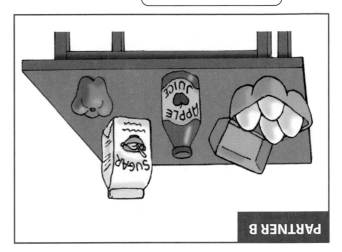

PARTNER B

 Write the ingredients for a recipe you know.

Recipe: _____
Ingredients:
_____
_____
_____
_____
_____

P **Complete each statement or question with the correct form of the verb.**

1. I never _____ a jacket.
   wear / am wearing

2. I _____ white shirts.
   like / am liking

3. Who _____ a suit today?
   wears / is wearing

4. How many sweaters do you _____ for your trip?
   need / needing

5. This afternoon we _____ shopping.
   going / 're going

PAIR WORK • *Exchange real information about your plans for the future.*

Start like this: What would you like to do in the next year?

Ideas
- move
- graduate
- have children
- get married

Q Suggest a remedy for each person in the pictures. Use **should** or **shouldn't**.

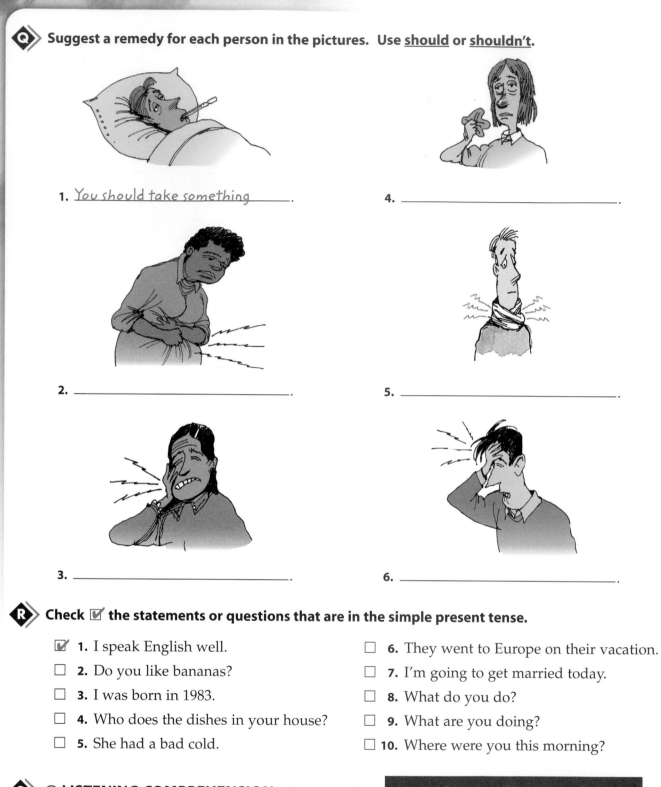

1. _You should take something_.

4. _____.

2. _____.

5. _____.

3. _____.

6. _____.

R Check ☑ the statements or questions that are in the simple present tense.

☑ **1.** I speak English well.

☐ **2.** Do you like bananas?

☐ **3.** I was born in 1983.

☐ **4.** Who does the dishes in your house?

☐ **5.** She had a bad cold.

☐ **6.** They went to Europe on their vacation.

☐ **7.** I'm going to get married today.

☐ **8.** What do you do?

☐ **9.** What are you doing?

☐ **10.** Where were you this morning?

S 🎧 **LISTENING COMPREHENSION.** Listen to the conversations. Check ☑ **Past**, **Present**, or **Future**. Then listen again to check your work.

	Past	Present	Future
1.	☐	☑	☐
2.	☐	☐	☐
3.	☐	☐	☐
4.	☐	☐	☐
5.	☐	☐	☐
6.	☐	☐	☐

Write a question for each response.

1. **A:** <u>Would you like coffee or tea</u>_____?
   B: Me? I'd like coffee, please.

2. **A:** _____?
   B: I'd like to go to Italy.

3. **A:** _____?
   B: I was born in New York.

4. **A:** _____?
   B: Yes, I ski very well.

5. **A:** _____?
   B: Me? I'm a morning person.

6. **A:** _____?
   B: I'm going to study German.

7. **A:** _____?
   B: I broke my arm!

U **Complete each sentence with a form of <u>be</u> or <u>have</u>.**

1. My daughter _____ long, blonde hair.
2. My parents _____ both short.
3. Salma Hayek _____ beautiful.
4. What color eyes _____ your children _____?
5. I _____ not very tall and not very short.

V **GROUP WORK.** On a separate piece of paper, write a physical description of yourself. Mix papers with your classmates. Then, guess who wrote each description.

I am tall. I have straight, brown hair.

PAIR WORK • *Exchange real information about a good or bad vacation.*

💡*Ideas*

Ask:
• When did you go?
• Where did you go?
• What happened?

Alphabetical word list

This is an alphabetical list of all productive vocabulary in the *Top Notch Fundamentals* units. The numbers refer to the page on which the word first appears or is defined. When a word has two meanings, both are in the list.

A

a 4
a lot of 54
A.M. 36
abdomen 102
ability 109
academic subject 117
across 20
across from 52
across the street 20
activity 68
actor 6
actress 18
actually 49
add 90
address 16
affirmative 4
after 68
afternoon 41
ago 92
ailment 104
airport 24
alphabet 8
always 72
an 4
ankle 102
any 84
apartment 52
apple 84
appliance 56
April 40
architect 4
architecture 117
arm 102
around the corner 20
around the corner from 52
article 4
artist 4
at 41
athlete 6
August 40
autumn 96
awful 57

B

back 102
backache 104
badly 109
bag 87
balcony 52
bald 100
ball 74
banana 84
bank 20
banker 4
baseball 42

base form 94
bath 68
bathroom 54
bathtub 56
be 4
be going to 119
beach 95
beans 84
beard 100
beautiful 48
beautifully 109
bed 56
bedroom 54
before 68
better 105
between 52
bike riding 95
birth 116
birthday 40
black 48
blonde 100
blouse 44
blue 48
boat 98
body 102
boil 90
bookcase 56
bookstore 20
born 116
boss 12
bottle 87
bowl 90
box 87
bread 86
break 102
breakfast 68
brother 28
brown 48
brush 68
building 52
burn 102
bus 22
bus station 22
business 117
busy 71
butter 86

C

cabbage 90
cabinet 56
calendar 39
camping 120
can *n.* 87
can *v.* 108
can't 108
car 108
cell phone 17

chair 56
check *v.* 70
cheese 86
chef 6
chest 102
chicken 86
child 28
childhood 116
chin 100
chop 90
chore 70
city, cities 36
class 37
classmate 12
clean *adj.* 48
clean *v.* 70
close 112
closet 54
clothes 44
cloudy 76
coffee 86
cold 76
colleague 12
color 48
comb 68
come 69
come home 68
common noun 9
community 20
computer 56
concert 38
congratulations 119
container 87
contraction 4
convenience store 20
cook 90
cool 76
corner 20
cough 104
could 112
count noun 84
crawl 114
cup 90
curly 100
cut 102
cute 32

D

daily 68
dance 108
dancing 73
dark 100
date 40
daughter 28
day 38
day after tomorrow 80

December 40
definitely 69
dentist 104
describe 32
descriptive adjective 48
desk 56
die 118
dining room 54
dinner 73
directions 20
dirty 48
dish 70
divorced 118
do 70
doctor 4
door 52
down 20
downstairs 54
down the street 20
drain 90
draw 108
dress 44
dressed 68
dresser 56
drink 86
drive *n.* 95
drive *v.* 24

E

ear 100
earache 104
early 37
easy chair 56
eat 68
education 117
egg 84
elevator 52
e-mail 70
engineer 4
engineering 117
evening 41
evening person 69
event 38
every 70
every day 70
exercise 70
expensive 110
explorer 122
eye 100
eyebrow 100
eyelash 100

F

face 100
factory 52
fall *v.* 102

fall *n.* 96
fall down 102
familiar 101
family 28
family member 28
father 28
favor 113
February 40
feed 79
feel 105
fever 104
few 114
finger 102
fingernail 102
first 40
first floor 52
first name 14
fish 86
fishing 120
fix 108
flight attendant 4
floor 52
food 84
foot 102
free time 120
freezer 56
frequency adverb 72
Friday 38
fridge 85
friend 12
furniture 56

G

game 38
garage 52
garbage 70
garden 52
garlic 90
get 68
get up 68
glasses 112
go 22
good-looking 32
go out 73
go to bed 68
graduate 116
grandchild 28
granddaughter 28
grandfather 28
grandmother 28
grandparent 28
grandson 28
gray 48
great 57
green 48
grow up 116

stadium 24
stairway 52
stomach 102
stomachache 104
stove 56
straight 22
straight (hair) 100
street 20
student 4
study 116
subject pronoun 6
sugar 86
suit 44
summer 96
Sunday 38
sunny 76
sweater 44
swim 108
swimming 95

T

table 56
tablespoon 90
take 24
take a bath 68
take a nap 70
take a shower 68
take a taxi 24
take out the garbage 70
take something 104

take the bus 24
take the train 24
tall 32
taxi 22
taxi stand 22
tea 86
teacher 4
teeth 68
telephone 56
temperature 76
terrible 57
terribly 109
that 44
their 12
there are 54
there is 21
these 44
they 6
thin 90
thing 89
third 40
third floor 52
this 44
this (afternoon) 80
those 44
throw 114
Thursday 38
tie 44
time 36
tired 110

title 14
today 80
toe 102
toenail 102
toilet 56
tomato 84
tomorrow 80
tongue 100
tonight 80
too 110
tooth 100
toothache 104
train 22
train station 22
transportation 25
travel 120
travel agency 20
Tuesday 38
turn left 22
turn off 112
turn on 112
turn right 22
TV 56
twice 70
typical 71

U

ugly 57
undressed 68
upstairs 54
usually 72

V

vacation 97
very 32
violin 108

W

wake 94
walk *n.* 95
walk *v.* 24
want 46
warm 76
was 92
wash 70
wash the dishes 70
watch TV 68
water 86
wavy 100
we 6
wear 94
weather 76
Wednesday 38
week 38
weekday 38
weekend 38
well 109
were 92
what 16
what day 38
what time 38
when 38

where 21
white 48
who 29
wife 28
window 52
windy 76
winter 96
wishes 119
woman 28
word 114
workplace 52
would like 87
write 94
writer 6

Y

year 40
yellow 48
yes 7
yes / no question 46
yesterday 92
you 6
young 32
your 12

Z

zero 16
Zodiac sign 42

Social language list

Welcome to *Top Notch!*

Hi.
Hello.
I'm [Martin].
Nice to meet you [too].
Glad to meet you.
It's a pleasure to meet you.
Good morning.
Good afternoon.
Good evening.

How's everything?
How's it going?
How are you?
[I'm] fine, thanks.
Great.
Not bad.
So-so.
And you?
I'm fine.

Good-bye.
Bye-bye.
See you later.
Take care.
Good night.
See you tomorrow.
OK.

Unit 1

What do you do?
I'm [a banker].
And you?
Excuse me. (to initiate a conversation)
Are you [Marie]?

No, I'm not. / Yes, I am.
Right over there.
Thank you.
You're welcome.
Hello.

I'm [John Bello].
Excuse me? (to ask someone to repeat)
How do you spell that?

Unit 2

[Tom], this is [Paula].
[Paula]'s my [classmate].
What's your [last name], please?

And your [first name]?
My [first name]? (to ask for clarification)
What's your phone number?

That's right.

Unit 3

Where's [the bookstore]? It's [down the street]. Is there a [bank] near here? Yes. There's a [bank] [down the street].	How do I get to the [train station]? Turn [right] at the corner. Go straight. Go to the corner of [Main Street] and 　[Park Avenue].	Go [two] blocks and turn [left]. No problem. Don't [walk]. Take [the bus].

Unit 4

Who's that? That's [my father]. And who are [they]? [They're] my [sisters], [Julie] and [Trish].	I have [one brother] and [two sisters]. Really? How old [is] your [brother]? Tell me about [your father].	Well, [he]'s a [doctor]. [He]'s very [tall]. And how about [your mother]?

Unit 5

What time is it? It's [one o'clock]. What time is [English class]? Uh-oh. (to express dismay) Am I late? No, you're not. Don't worry.	You're on time. What day is the [party]? There's a [play] on [Tuesday]. Would you like to go? Sounds great. What time? OK. (to express willingness)	Let's meet at [a quarter to seven]. When's [your birthday]? On [July 15th]. When's yours? My birthday's in [November].

Unit 6

I like that [dress]. Do you like this [sweater]? Yes, I do. / No, I don't.	Actually, I think [it's] [very nice]. Let's go shopping. What do you need?	I need [a tie] and [a new suit]. Is that all?

Unit 7

I [study] at [the Park School]. Where's that? On [Second Street]. Near [the mall]. Do you live nearby? What about you?	Me? I [work] at [Peter's Restaurant]. Do you live in a house or an apartment? What's it like? Well, there are [three bedrooms] and 　[a large kitchen].	Sounds nice. Look at that [easy chair]. What do you think? You do? Definitely. I'm not sure.

Unit 8

Are you a morning person or an evening 　person? I'm definitely [an evening person]. Why do you say that? I get up [after ten].	I go to bed [after two]. What's your typical [week] like? On [Mondays] and [Wednesdays] I [go 　to school]. Sounds like you're pretty busy.	Long time no see. Do you always [take the bus]? I usually [walk]. No wonder I never see you!

Unit 9

What's the weather like? I'm calling from [San Francisco]. How's the weather in [Buenos Aires]? Awful. No kidding. It's [hot and sunny] here. Hello? (to answer the telephone)	This is [Laura]. What are you doing? Should I call you back later? Talk to you later. Bye. So, what are you doing [this weekend]? If the weather is [good], I'm [meeting 　Andrea in the park].	Do you want to get together [on 　Sunday]? I'm not doing anything special. Sure. (to express willingness) Call me [Sunday morning].

Unit 10

How about some [tomato potato soup]? That sounds [delicious]! I love [tomatoes]. [Are] there any [potatoes] [on the shelf]? Do we have any [tomatoes]? I'll check.	Would you like [coffee] or [tea]? I'd like [coffee], please. No, thanks. Please pass the [butter]. Here you go. Hey, [Alison].	Would you like to join me? What are you [drinking]? Mmm. I think I'd like [the same thing].

Unit 11

Where were you [yesterday]?
When?
I was [at home].
There was a great [party] at [the Pike Museum].
There was?
Too bad I wasn't there!

Pretty good, thanks.
What did you do last weekend?
Not much.
I [went running].
About the same.
You look [great].
Were you on vacation?

Yes, I was.
I just got back [last week].
How was it?
Really nice.
It's great to see you.
Welcome back.

Unit 12

Who's that?
[She] look[s] familiar.
Who?
The [woman] with [long, curly, blonde] [hair].

That's [Daniela Mercury].
[She]'s a [singer] from [Brazil].
What happened?
I [broke] my [ankle].
I'm sorry to hear that.

I feel [awful].
What's wrong?
You really should [take something].
Good idea.
I hope you feel better.

Unit 13

Can you [swim]?
Can you?
I [swim] [very well].
When did you learn?
When I was [about eight].
Was it hard?

Not at all.
I'm really sorry.
I'm too busy.
I don't feel well.
It's too late.
I have other plans.

That's too bad.
Maybe some other time.
Could you do me a favor?
Could you please [close the window]?

Unit 14

Where were you born?
I was born in [New York].
And did you grow up there?
That's interesting.

Why did you move there?
My parents are [Canadian].
What's new?
I have some [great] news.

My [daughter] is going to [have a baby].
Congratulations.
What do you like to do in your free time?

Countries and nationalities

Country	Nationality	Country	Nationality	Country	Nationality
Argentina	Argentinian / Argentine	France	French	Peru	Peruvian
Australia	Australian	Germany	German	The Philippines	Filipino
Bolivia	Bolivian	Greece	Greek	Poland	Polish
Brazil	Brazilian	Guatemala	Guatemalan	Russia	Russian
Canada	Canadian	Indonesia	Indonesian	Saudi Arabia	Saudi / Saudi Arabian
Chile	Chilean	Ireland	Irish	Spain	Spanish
China	Chinese	Japan	Japanese	Switzerland	Swiss
Colombia	Colombian	Korea	Korean	Thailand	Thai
Costa Rica	Costa Rican	Lebanon	Lebanese	Turkey	Turkish
Ecuador	Ecuadorian	Malaysia	Malaysian	The United Kingdom	British
Egypt	Egyptian	Mexico	Mexican	The United States	American
El Salvador	El Salvadoran	New Zealand	New Zealander	Venezuela	Venezuelan
England	English	Panama	Panamanian	Uruguay	Uruguayan

Numbers 100 to 1,000,000,000

100	one hundred	10,000	ten thousand
500	five hundred	100,000	one hundred thousand
1,000	one thousand	1,000,000	one million
5,000	five thousand	1,000,000,000	one billion

Verb list

This is an alphabetical list of all active verbs in the *Top Notch Fundamentals* units.
The page numbers refer to the page on which the base form of the verb first appears.

base form	simple past	page	base form	simple past	page	base form	simple past	page
be	was / were	4	get	got	68	play	played	70
ride	rode	95	go	went	22	put	put	90
break	broke	102	graduate	graduated	116	read	read	70
brush	brushed	68	grow	grew	116	relax	relaxed	120
burn	burned	102	hand	handed	112	ride	rode	94
can	could	108	hang out	hung out	120	see	saw	94
check	checked	70	have	had	30	sew	sewed	108
clean	cleaned	70	help	helped	112	shave	shaved	68
close	closed	112	hurt	hurt	102	ski	skied	108
comb	combed	68	knit	knitted	108	sleep	slept	120
come	came	69	laugh	laughed	114	spell	spelled	9
cut	cut	102	lie	lay	104	study	studied	116
dance	danced	108	like	liked	45	swim	swam	108
die	died	118	listen	listened	70	take	took	24
do	did	70	live	lived	118	travel	traveled	120
draw	drew	108	make	made	73	turn	turned	22
drive	drove	24	move	moved	116	wake	woke	94
eat	ate	68	mow	mowed	74	walk	walked	24
exercise	exercised	70	need	needed	46	want	wanted	46
fall	fell	102	open	opened	112	wash	washed	70
feed	fed	79	paint	painted	108	watch	watched	68
feel	felt	105	pass	passed	87	wear	wore	94
fix	fixed	108	pick up	picked up	114	write	wrote	94

Pronunciation table

These are the pronunciation symbols used in *Top Notch Fundamentals*.

Vowels		Consonants			
Symbol	Key Words	Symbol	Key Words	Symbol	Key Words
i	feed	p	park, happy	ʃ	she, station,
ɪ	did	b	back, cabbage		special, discussion
eɪ	date, table	t	tie	ʒ	leisure
ɛ	bed, neck	d	die	h	hot, who
æ	bad, hand	k	came, kitchen, quarter	m	men
ɑ	box, father	g	game, go	n	sun, know
ɔ	wash	ʧ	chicken, watch	ŋ	sung, singer
oʊ	comb, post	ʤ	jacket, orange	w	week, white
ʊ	book, good	f	face, photographer	l	light, long
u	boot, food, student	v	vacation	r	rain, writer
ʌ	but, mother	θ	thing, math	y	yes, use, music
ə	banana, mustache	ð	then, that		
ɚ	shirt, birthday	s	city, psychology		
aɪ	cry, eye	z	please, goes		
aʊ	about, how	t̬	butter, bottle		
ɔɪ	boy	t˺	button		
ɪr	here, near				
ɛr	chair				
ɑr	guitar, are				
ɔr	door, chore				
ʊr	tour				

VOCABULARY BOOSTER

UNIT 1

🎧 More occupations

1. an accountant

2. a bank teller

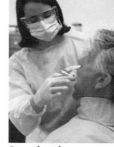
3. a dentist

4. an electrician

5. a florist

6. a gardener

7. a grocery clerk

8. a hairdresser

9. a mechanic

10. a pharmacist

11. a professor

12. a reporter

13. a salesperson

14. a travel agent

15. a secretary

16. a waiter

UNIT 2

🎧 More relationships

1. a supervisor
2. an employee

3. a teammate

🎧 More titles

1. Doctor [Smith] OR Dr. [Smith]

2. Professor [Brown]

3. Captain [Jones]

UNIT 3
🎧 More places in the community

1. a clothing store

2. an electronics store

3. a fire station

4. a police station

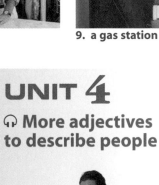
5. a shoe store

6. a toy store

7. a video store

8. a dry cleaners

9. a gas station

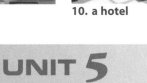
10. a hotel

11. a supermarket

UNIT 4
🎧 More adjectives to describe people

1. slim / thin

2. muscular

3. heavy

UNIT 5
🎧 More events

1. an exhibition

2. the opera

3. the ballet

4. a football game

5. a volleyball game

6. a baseball game

UNIT 6
🎧 More clothes

1. bathing suits / swimsuits

2. a bathrobe

3. boots

4. a coat

5. a hat

8. a nightgown

9. a raincoat
10. an umbrella

6. a shirt
7. jeans

11. sandals

12. pajamas

13. a T-shirt
14. shorts

15. socks

16. pantyhose

17. underwear

UNIT 7

More home and office vocabulary

1. a fence
2. a driveway
3. a roof

4. an intercom

5. a doorbell

6. a fire escape

7. a pillow

8. a blanket
9. a sheet

10. a medicine cabinet
11. toothpaste
12. a toothbrush

15. towels

16. a faucet

13. a shower curtain
14. a bath mat

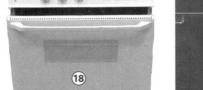

17. a burner
18. an oven

19. a dishwasher

V 4

20. a coffee maker

21. a ladle
22. a pot

23. a food processor

24. a napkin
25. a place mat
26. a glass

27. a bowl
28. a plate
29. a cup
30. a saucer

31. a fork
32. a knife
33. a tablespoon / a soup spoon
34. a teaspoon

35. a filing cabinet

36. a fax machine

UNIT 8
⌒ More household chores

1. dust

2. sweep

3. mop

4. vacuum

UNIT 9
🎧 More weather

1. a thunderstorm

2. a snowstorm

3. a hurricane

4. a tornado

UNIT 10
🎧 More vegetables

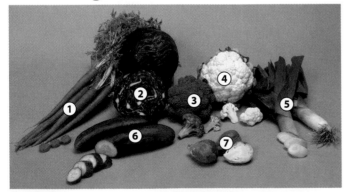

1. carrots
2. cabbage
3. broccoli
4. cauliflower
5. leeks
6. cucumbers
7. brussels sprouts

9. lettuce
10. asparagus
11. an eggplant
12. beans
13. peas
14. celery

8. corn

15. garlic

⌒ More fruits

1. a tangerine
2. a grapefruit
3. a lemon
4. a lime
5. an orange

6. grapes
7. a pineapple
8. bananas

9. a pear

10. apricots

11. peaches

12. strawberries

13. raspberries

14. a honeydew melon
15. an avocado
16. a papaya
17. a mango
18. a kiwi

19. a watermelon

20. raisins
21. figs
22. prunes
23. dates

UNIT 11
⌒ More weekend activities

1. go horseback riding

2. go sailing

3. play golf

4. go rollerblading

5. go snorkeling

6. go rock climbing

7. go ice skating

8. go windsurfing

UNIT 12

🎧 More parts of the body

1. knuckle
2. wrist

3. calf
4. thigh
5. elbow

UNIT 13

🎧 More musical instruments

1. a cello

2. a piano

3. a tuba

4. a trumpet

5. a trombone

6. a flute

7. a clarinet

8. a recorder

9. a guitar

10. a saxophone

11. a xylophone

12. an accordion

13. drums

UNIT 14

🎧 More academic subjects

1. biology

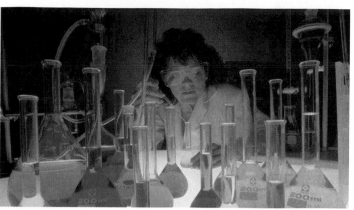
2. chemistry

3. history

4. fine art

5. drama

🎧 More free-time activities

1. go skiing

2. go hiking

3. play

4. garden

5. go on a cruise

6. get a manicure

🎧 TOP NOTCH POP LYRICS 🎵

Excuse Me, Please [Unit 2]
(CHORUS)

Excuse me—please excuse me.
What's your number?
What's your name?
I would love to get to know you,
and I hope you feel the same.

I'll give you my e-mail address.
Write to me at my dot-com.
You can send a note in English
so I'll know who it came from.

Excuse me—please excuse me.
Was that 0078?
Well, I think the class is starting,
and I don't want to be late.

But it's really nice to meet you.
I'll be seeing you again.
Just call me on my cell phone
when you're looking for a friend.

(CHORUS)

So welcome to the classroom.
There's a seat right over there.
I'm sorry, but you're sitting in
our teacher's favorite chair!

Excuse me—please excuse me.
What's your number?
What's your name?

Tell Me All about It [Unit 4]
Tell me about your father.
He's a doctor and he's very tall.
And how about your mother?
She's a lawyer. That's her picture on
    the wall.

Tell me about your brother.
He's an actor, and he's twenty-three.
And how about your sister?
She's an artist. Don't you think she looks
    like me?

(CHORUS)

Tell me about your family—
who they are and what they do.
Tell me all about it.
It's so nice to talk with you.

Tell me about your family.
I have a brother and a sister, too.
And what about your parents?
Dad's a teacher, and my mother's eyes
    are blue.

(CHORUS)

Who's the pretty girl in that photograph?
That one's me!
You look so cute!
Oh, that picture makes me laugh!
And who are the people there, right below
    that one?
Let me see … that's my mom and dad.
They both look very young.

(CHORUS)

Tell me all about it.
Tell me all about it.

On the Weekend [Unit 8]
(CHORUS)

On the weekend,
when we go out,
there is always so much joy and laughter.
On the weekend,
we never think about
the days that come before and after.

He gets up every morning.
Without warning, the bedside clock rings
    the alarm.
So he gets dressed—
he does his best to be on time.
He combs his hair, goes down the stairs,
and makes some breakfast.
A bite to eat, and he feels fine.
Yes, he's on his way
to one more working day.

(CHORUS)

On Thursday night,
when he comes home from work,
he gets undressed, and if his room's a mess,
he cleans the house. Sometimes he takes
    a rest.
Maybe he cooks something delicious,
and when he's done
he washes all the pots and dishes,
then goes to bed.
He knows the weekend's just ahead.

(CHORUS)

My Favorite Day [Unit 11]
Last night we walked together.
It seems so long ago.
And we just talked and talked.
Where did the time go?

We saw the moonlit ocean
across the sandy beach.
The waves of summer fell,
barely out of reach.

(CHORUS)

Yes, that was then,
and this is now,
and all I do is think about
yesterday,
my favorite day of the week.

When I woke up this morning,
my feelings were so strong.
I put my pen to paper,
and I wrote this song.

I'm glad I got to know you.
You really made me smile.
My heart belonged to you
for a little while.

(CHORUS)

It was wonderful to be with you.
We had so much to say.
It was awful when we waved good-bye.
Why did it end that way?

(CHORUS)

I Wasn't Born Yesterday [Unit 14]
I went to school and learned the lessons
of the human heart.
I got an education in
psychology and art.

It doesn't matter what you say.
I know the silly games you play.

(CHORUS)

I wasn't born yesterday.
I wasn't born yesterday.

Well, pretty soon I graduated
with a good degree.
It took some time to understand
the way you treated me,

and it's too great a price to pay.
I've had enough, and anyway,

(CHORUS)

So you think I'd like to marry you
and be your pretty wife?
Well, that's too bad, I'm sorry, now.
Grow up and get a life!

It doesn't matter what you say.
I know the silly games you play.

(CHORUS)